Y0-CXJ-011

Lynette,

thank you for the Love you Shower on me like I'm really your daughter! Thank you for all that you add to my life especially the Laughter!

It's that Simple!

Love
Theresa

IT'S THAT SIMPLE

THERESA KIRK

Foreword by

D. L. Hughley

Copyright by Theresa Kirk 2017

All rights reserved. No part of this book may be reproduced by any mechanical, photographic, or electronic process, or in the form of a phonographic recording; nor may it be stored in a retrieval system, transmitted, or otherwise copied for public or private use without written permission from the publisher.

ISBN: 978-0-9993455-2-8
Library of Congress Control Number: 2010938173
Edited by: Michelle Otis
Library Director: Sandra L. Slayton

Front and Back Cover Design: Juan Roberts, Creative Lunacy, Inc.
Interior Design: James Sparkman, Sparkman Designs

Published by:

Knowledge Power Books
A Division of Knowledge Power Communications Inc.
Valencia, CA 91355
www.knowledgepowerbooks.com

Printed in the United States of America

PRELUDE

It's That Simple is the fourth book of the *Some Things Made Plain* series. The series is now complete. When I started this writing project it was my desire, inspired by the Holy Spirit, to take scripture and make it plain to the reader who believes that the Bible is a big book with 66 chapters and is challenging to read.

This final title alone makes me believe that I have achieved just that. In this volume, you will read devotions like, *Always Unfailing*, *2 Will Do*, and one of my favorites, *Quintessential*. This devotion speaks to the necessity of Christ as our Savior—Jesus *is* essential. Another favorite is titled *Bully*. Our adversary the devil is just that—a bully.

My prayer is that coupling these devotions with your daily Bible reading will give you a simple understanding of our Lord's heart towards each of us, that His desires fully come to life in your heart and mind. Scripture was written for our living and learning. It is not a daunting task but a beautiful journey about love and relationship inspired by the One who created us, simply because He loves us.

It's that Simple Author,

Theresa Kirk

DEDICATION

I dedicate this volume, *It's That Simple* to every reader who picks up any book I have written and for every book I will write. Thank you! I have enjoyed writing every page but more importantly, I have appreciated my time with the Holy Spirit, which is creativity at its best. I thank God that He decided to let me in so that I can have witty ideas to complete this series.

Willa Robinson, thank you for taking my first manuscript without reading one word. I will always remember our first date together, where I knew after our lunch that day we'd be friends forever. You are a real gem, and I am honored to know you. Thank you for your wisdom, your faith, your commitment to Vernon's well-being, your strength as a woman, your laugh, and your friendship. I love you; this one is for you.

It's That Simple.

~ Theresa Kirk

TABLE OF CONTENTS

Mom,
You did it. You completed your series.
All those days that you had to write are over. Congrats!
More books to come, I'm sure, but today cherish what
you have just accomplished.

~ Jaylon K.

Mom,
Congratulations on your fourth book.
I am so proud of you, and love you so much.
Blanché, thank you for sharing your journey with us
along the way.

~ Chelsea

FOREWORD

These Devotionals were right on time when I needed them!

~ D.L. Hughley

I have had the pleasure of intimately knowing this amazing author Theresa Kirk for well over 20 years! During this time, I have seen many changes, as anyone would in 20 years, and the one thing that I can count on is her love of God, family, and friends.

When Theresa embarked upon stepping out on faith and writing her very first book *Some Things Made Plain* six years ago, I was overjoyed and full of encouragement and support. Just as she committed all of herself to that project, she has done the very same with this current masterpiece *It's That Simple.*

Theresa's love for God is infectious and truly a wonder to watch and read! She is a committed friend and mother who always rules on the side of excellence. While reading this amazing book, remember to let the pages leap into your very soul, because it was written just for you!

Theresa Kirk, we are so proud and happy for you!

~ LaDonna Hughley

Simply Grace

PRAISE FOR SIMPLICITY

The title says it all: it's that simple. Theresa has a unique gift to simplify the Word of God, making it easy to implement the life-changing principles in your daily life. She's more than an author, teacher, motivational speaker, minister, and mother—she's an inspirational artist. Her words are visual; they become images in your mind. They have a way of jumping off the pages and into your hearts. Each book in this series is not only on time for each season of the reader's life but with each book, you feel Theresa's growth in her own life. As a reader, I've grown with her as I read each book, and this one is no different. Simply put, this book is the perfect end to not only this series but a chapter of life. I'm excited to see what God will download into Theresa in this new chapter and season of her life. I'm so blessed to have her on speed dial and to know that she's not only my mentor, friend, teacher, and rider, she's my *SISTER!* I love you, Mack, and I'm so godly proud of you, not just for the completion of this book, but for the way you have made you a priority, because you are worth it and more!

– Brandi Reneé Allen

"It's that simple," is what she would say to me in most of our sessions. I had the pleasure and pain of being coached by Minister Theresa Kirk. She has acquired the art of transforming the body and mind. Her ability to teach the art of healthy eating and exercise is a challenge for most. To be coached by someone who has obtained this art has been a blessing for me. Theresa has many techniques that you will love and hate, but the one I *LOVE* is her direct way to encourage you as she challenges you to become your best you. The experience has been one of true transformation emotionally, mentally, and physically. I finally made a decision to be committed to me. I believe she's onto something when she says, "It's that simple." This simplistic way of teaching has been beneficial in my personal process. Something amazing is coming out of this book; I can feel it. Millions will be blessed—millions.

– Felicia Houston

When Theresa asked me to write a blurb for her book, I had no idea what to write. However, as I started reviewing the pages of the book, I began to reminisce about our first meeting and our journey together since that meeting. I instantly knew there was something special about Theresa, aside from the fact that we dressed in the same color. And I was right.

She is one extraordinary woman. It wasn't long before we developed our author-publisher relationship, but she is my friend. My husband and I have unofficially adopted her as our daughter. I think I may be her oldest friend. However, she relates to me with ultimate respect and love. We find so much to laugh about because she is a comedian and an actress. I have learned so much from her. Theresa is intelligent, resourceful, wise, witty, loving, and lovable. I love how she cares and loves her children and her family. The Lord has blessed her with many gifts; one is a miraculous gift of recognizing and using the smallest miracle or greatest pain to teach on how to understand God and the Bible better. She uses her tragedies, sorrows, and laughter and finds a teaching moment. *It's That Simple* is another demonstration of her gift. Readers will be blessed. Thank you, my daughter, for using your gift to teach me and others.

– Willa Robinson

ABOVE THY NAME

Psalms 138:2 (KJV)

I will worship toward thy holy temple,
and praise thy name for thy loving kindness and for thy truth:
for thou hast magnified thy word above all thy name.

It is impossible to put the inspired, infallible Word of God on too high a pedestal, for God Himself honors it above His name! The Word is not greater than God for He wrote it by His Spirit, but it is greater than His name, which represents Him and all that He is and does. The Word, in fact, is His name revealed. The name of the Lord refers to the manifestation of His character and nature. God's Word refers to His promises to us. When others see these promises (prayers) answered, His name is exalted and He, yet again, is glorified in the earth. The *WORD* of God is good for doctrine, reproof, and correction, which is in righteousness for the purposes of God speaking on His own behalf to us for Him, for our good, and for the good of those around us.

Also, look at this great truth: *"In the beginning was the Word, and the Word was with God, and the Word was God. He was in the beginning with God." (John 1:1-2, NKJV)* God is clearly stating that He has put His only begotten Son above His own Name. Jesus is the Word. The creator of it all has made it plain just how much Jesus means to Him, and this should matter to us. Consider how many names of God there are. I have found over 625 and in this verse, He declares that He has personally put His Word above all of them. Here is a glimpse at some of His many names in hope that you will see just how extensive this declaration is: Elohim the self-existing one, Adonai Lord and Master, Nissi our banner, Jireh our provider, Shalom our peace, Tsidkenu our righteousness, Rohi our shepherd, just to name a few. The remarkable thing about this is that these names make up every scripture verse you will ever read. Again, His Word reveals His name, concluding that the self-existing one, who is our Lord and Master, is our true banner that provides peace coupled with righteousness. Yes, He is the good Shepherd. Magnified above all this, I too will worship toward His holy temple and praise His name for His loving kindness and for His truth.

"His Word is our bond."

THE BLOOD OF CHRIST

EPHESIANS 2:13 (NIV)

But now in Christ Jesus you who once were far away have been brought near by the blood of Christ.

THERE is one scene that is forever etched in my mind from a very popular medical television series. A couple was having a baby, but the pregnancy came with complications that required surgery. Before taking this very pregnant woman into surgery, her husband tells the surgeons, "If you can't save our baby, please do everything you can to save my wife. After all, we can make another baby, but she can't be replaced. She's the love of my life." There were complications during delivery, and the mother was dying. They had to focus on saving the baby, however, the doctor, whose care they had been under, had now become attached and wanted very much to honor the husband's request. In order to get her heart to pump, they needed more blood. It became utter chaos in the operating room. The surgeon was yelling over and over get more blood, but no one moved. The chief had entered and shouted, "It's over. There is no more blood."

I began to cry, not because of what was happening on this episode, but at the thought that what if we were told there was no more Blood? On the day Jesus rose from the dead, Mary Magdalene was there weeping at His tomb. Not recognizing Jesus, she asked Him, "Where have you taken the body?" With great excitement, she reached to touch Him. Jesus told her, *"Do not touch me, for I have not ascended to my Father."* What He was saying was His blood had not yet hit the mercy seat, and at that moment the bloodshed had not yet gained its full power. After all, it is a fact according to the Word that once Jesus' Blood hit the mercy seat, our sins were forgiven in an instant.

"His Blood gave us life."

COVER

JAMES 5:20 (ESV)

...let him know that whoever brings back a sinner from his wandering will save his soul from death and will cover a multitude of sins.

GOD'S word is not a book just for our reading, rather, it is for our living. When we claim to have faith in Him, we should be quick to share Him with others giving them a chance to get to know this ever-so-gracious God. James tells us that when we do this, and they accept Him as savior, we have just saved them from death as well as covered a multitude of sins. Essentially, we have just assisted in snatch- ing them from hell's door. Belief, faith, and trust must have hands and feet—ours. Remember, you were once in the same place. Thank God for the one He sent in the earth to recover you.

Cover: Insurance. To insure against risk or loss.

"We are recovery agents He chose."

DIVINE PERFECTION

ROMANS 1:20 (AMP)

*For since the creation of the world His invisible attributes,
His eternal power and divine nature, have been clearly seen,
being understood through what has been made...*

THE Trinity consists of Father, Son, and Holy Spirit. There are three qualities of the universe: time, space, and matter. To exist (except for God), all three are required. Each quality consists of three elements. Let us take a closer look at this amazing number in its Divine Perfection.

Man is made of three parts:
BODY · SOUL · SPIRIT

Human abilities are three:
THOUGHT · WORD · DEED

The divine attributes are threefold:
OMNISCIENT · OMNIPRESENT · OMNIPOTENT

He is:
HOLY · RIGHTEOUS · JUST

(1 JOHN 5:8) Three bear witness:
SPIRIT · WATER · BLOOD

Christ is three shepards:
THE GOOD SHEPHERD
Speaking of His death. (JOHN 10:14-15)
THE GREAT SHEPHERD
Speaking of His resurrection. (HEBREWS 13:10)
THE CHIEF SHEPHERD
Speaking of His glory. (1 PETER 5:4)

The three appearances of Christ:
PAST
Has appeared to put away sin (HEBREWS 9:26)
PRESENT
Is appearing in the presence of God (HEBREWS 9:24)
FUTURE
Will appear to those who await Him (HEBREWS 9:28)

"One Father, One Holy Spirit, One Christ, Divine Perfection."

EVERLASTING

Ephesians 1:7 (NIV)

In him we have redemption through his blood, the forgiveness of sins, in accordance with the riches of God's grace

Jesus' blood cleanses our sin

"But if we walk in the light, as He is in the light, we have fellowship with one another, and the blood of Jesus, his Son, cleanses us from all sin" (1 John 1:7).

Jesus' blood sets us apart

"And so Jesus also suffered outside the city gate to make the people holy through his own blood" (Hebrews 13:12). Sanctification means "to be set apart," and the application of Jesus' blood sets believers apart as God's very own.

Christ's blood grants us access into God's presence

"Therefore, brothers and sisters, since we have confidence to enter the Most Holy Place by the blood of Jesus..." (Hebrews 10:19). So, friends, we can now—without hesitation—walk right up to God, into "the Most Holy Place." Jesus has cleared the way by the blood of His sacrifice, acting as our priest before God. The 'curtain' into God's presence is his body.

Jesus' blood defends the guilty

"...and all are justified freely by his grace through the redemption that came by Christ Jesus" (Romans 3:24).

Jesus' blood brings peace

At Jesus' birth, the heavenly host promised peace to men. In one way or another, everyone is looking for peace. The Scriptures declare that genuine and lasting peace is only available through Jesus' blood: *"...making peace through his blood, shed on the cross" (Colossians 1:20).*

"The power of the Blood is everlasting."

FAITHFUL

DEUTERONOMY 7:9 (AMPC)

Know, recognize, and understand therefore that the Lord your God, He is God, the faithful God, Who keeps covenant and steadfast love and mercy with those who love Him and keep His commandments, to a thousand generations...

"*To a thousand generations*" What a pledge and promise from our faithful God! All we must do is stay in line with His Word. Faithful, dependable, obedient, affectionate, and reliable are what God our Father has committed to be to each of His children. Steadfast, changeless, and dedicated is His love for us. He said His love is steadfast, that means that it never changes. He is committed to loving us forever. His amazing faithfulness it is a covenant which includes every generation from here to eternity. Can you think of anyone else in your life who could possibly keep such a promise? Jesus has become the mediator of a new covenant *(HEBREWS 8:6)* in which the love of God is even more strongly expressed. In it, God continues to commit Himself to be our God if we will be His people. The solid reason we can trust that His faithfulness will never cease is God made it plain when He said He is not a man that He should lie *(NUMBERS 23:19). "Heaven and earth shall pass away, but my words shall not pass away" (MATTHEW 24:35, KJV).* His Word He has even put above His name. His Word includes this very scripture that declares steadfast love, mercy, and lastly His faithfulness toward us. God is faithful to keep His promises. We can count on Him. We may fail Him, but, He will not fail us.

"Faithful is the God in Heaven."

GOD

JOHN 15:13 (NKJV)

Greater love has no one than this,
than to lay down one's life for his friends.

WHAT HE DID

Justified us before His Father
Emancipated us, making us joint heirs
Salvaged us from the eternal grave of hell
Unshackled us from Satan's chains that had us bound
Set us **Free** from our iniquitous past
Gave His life as a **Ransom** for us

WHO HE IS

Compassionate—daily makes intercession for us
Healer—by every stripe He took on His back *WE ARE HEALED*
Incomparable—none like Him in all the earth
Savior—His blood on the mercy seat granted us
Grace, **Salvation**, and **Eternal Life** **Tender**—He bore our griefs

WHY HE DID IT

LOVE

"Love the greatest gift ever given."

HOLY SPIRIT

2 CORINTHIANS 13:14 (KJV)

The grace of the Lord Jesus Christ, and the love of God, and the communion of the Holy Ghost, be with you all. Amen.

MOST of us would say we want to live a victorious Christian life, but without daily communion with the Holy Spirit, it's impossible to attain that goal. Communion with the Holy Spirit is the launching pad for a life of supernatural power and consistency. As a leader in ministry, my success will be based on my ability to rely on assistance from the Holy Spirit. Jesus, the one true Son of God, even explained that He does nothing apart from the Father, therefore, He does only what He sees the Father doing. Jesus gave us this answer, *"Very truly I tell you, the Son can do nothing by himself; he can do only what he sees his Father doing, because whatever the Father does the Son also does"* *(JOHN 5:19, NIV)*. God, in His infinite wisdom, set up all those whom He loves for success in every area of our lives, however, for this plan to work, we must be in communion with Him daily. In his first letter to the Corinthians, Paul tells us that unless the Spirit of the Lord lets us in on the deep things of God, we will not have such wisdom *(2:9-12)*. In order for any person to function actively in any capacity of ministry or career, they must be led by the Holy Spirit.

At the onset of my career with an elite women's retailer (specializing in lingerie), I prayed daily for the Holy Spirit to go before me to lead, govern, and guide to help me achieve my desired success. However, I must admit that after obtaining my goal—ten President's Club achievement awards and three promotions later—my ratings began to drop and my sales started to dwindle. I stopped to ask, "What has changed?" I clearly heard, "You stopped inviting me." While I understand work is not technically ministry, it was a clear example that for me to have God-ordained success, I must include Him in all my journeys. This includes my family, ministry, associations, and all my God-ordained assignments. To approach any ministry appointment without the Comforter's guidance, I would be setting myself and those attached to my charge up for failure.

"My success is based on my invitation for His Presence."

INCREDIBLE

ACTS 26:8 (KJV)

Why should it be thought a thing incredible with you, that God should raise the dead?

"CHELSEA, what one word comes to mind when you think of God?" "Incredible," she quickly replied. In search of my scripture for revelation to scribe this incredible God, I'm stuck only to find that there is only one scripture that utilizes this word, and it is found in *ACTS 26:8*. Therefore, in my quest to find out why, I went straight to the thesaurus.

In case you are wondering why this was so hard to grasp, let me explain. We are all guilty of saying just how incredible He is or how incredible are the things He does. The thesaurus gives synonyms such as absurd, far-fetched, flimsy, phony, suspect, questionable, and ridiculous. Would you agree that, in fact, He is none of the above? Luke, the author of the book of *ACTS*, was stating in this letter that Paul, at first a Pharisee now a believer of Jesus Christ, thought it strange that King Agrippa should marvel that such a big God could do amazing things like raise the dead. I would like to firmly state that there is truly nothing phony, suspect, questionable, or ridiculous about the Lord of heaven and earth. He is, however, Awesome, Holy, Gracious, Wonderful, Longsuffering, Faithful, Forgiving, and Just. Look at your life alone, has He not done so many incredible things; He saved you before the foundations were formed, that is incredible.

"Our incredible God deserves unbelievable praise."

JOY

NEHEMIAH (NIV)

...the joy of the Lord is your strength.

RECENTLY, I was faced with another opportunity to trust and believe that God will do what He said He would do on my behalf. I had to take my eyes off what I saw and do my best to shut my ears to negative words being spoken, that quite naturally were not lining up with the good word I had recently received from God. However, there is more to this strategy than my eyes and ears. I was also very careful about the words that I would speak. A good friend told me, "Thank you for being strong." I quickly responded, "The joy of the Lord is my strength," because the joy of the Lord is our strength!

We must remember who is letting us in on this vital information. There must be a secret to unlock for our benefit. Here it is: joy produces strength, and strength is needed to fight. We are called to *"fight the good fight of the faith" (1 TIMOTHY 6:12).* I sense that many people in the body of Christ are tired of fighting the good fight of the faith. They are struggling to fight because they have lost their joy.

Why is this strength critical? I propose two points: (1) Because in the midst of a fight, God knows the winner in us, and He carefully uses this opportunity to expose us to our self, and (2) once we are aware of this inner strength that was given from the Lord Himself, our Faith is increased. What makes me the expert? I'm not. I just find from my experience that at the end of the battle, as long as I stood firm I was able to see a different ending. At first glance, I saw defeat. However, because I stood, I had the chance to look at the champion in the mirror, not behind me but right in front.

PHILIPPIANS 4:4 says, *"Rejoice in the Lord always. I will say it again: Rejoice!"* How often are you to rejoice? You know the answer: Always! You are to rejoice always, because joy is the easiest fruit to lose. You can't live off of the joy you had yesterday. Joy can give you strength only when you possess it. Why does James tell us to count it pure joy whenever we face trials? Because joy gives you strength to fight your trials, and if you'll fight through the trials, you will overcome. James continues, *"Let perseverance finish its work so that you may be mature and complete, not lacking anything" (1:4).* James has in mind victory over trials, not acceptance of trials.

"The Lord is my joy in Him I find strength."

KEPT

ISAIAH 26:3 (NIV)

You will keep in perfect peace
those whose minds are steadfast,
because they trust in you.

I GAVE a few of my girlfriends a letter from the alphabet, Lisa's letter was *K.* She chose the word *kept.* Her reason? In her own words, she wrote, "With God I am a *KEPT WOMAN.* I want for nothing. All my needs are met through His love and grace. He showers me with love and attention. He is my provider and my faith in Him does not waver." What a confidence that her choice word is kept! This tells me that she has had a few experiences with this promise keeper. She uttered these words with backbone. To speak with such brashness is only made possible from real life experiences, such as a loss, a lack of direction, some form of disappointment, or even a celebration where you called on Him and He answered expeditiously. His prompt awareness of our need of Him builds this trustworthy relationship. What a revelation! Because of God's unchanging love and mighty power, we can adjust our attitude to be steady and stable, unwavering in times of turmoil or uncertainty, simply because He promised to keep us always. Being kept by God has another level to this great partnership. In *1 CORINTHIANS 1:8,* Paul declares that He will keep you strong to the end so you will be free from all blame on the day when our Lord Jesus Christ returns. This partnership was mandated by the Lord who created us to love forever.

"Being kept by One who never breaks a promise."

LOVE

Romans 8:35 (KJV)

Who shall separate us from the love of Christ? Shall tribulation, or distress, or persecution, or famine, or nakedness, or peril, or sword?

How befitting that my beautiful friend quickly responded to my word request. Carnetta is one whom I would say the two of us together could have easily been hippies. We would have fit right into the flower child era, where everything was about love and peace.

Paul is expressing here that no matter what comes our way, it will always work out in our favor. God is not going to allow anything to go to waste. You know this well if you're a parent. We tell our kids, "Don't waste your food. I paid for that with my hard-earned money." God is saying, "I paid for your life with my life through my only Son." Therefore, there is nothing that that can separate us from Him, nothing. Tribulation can also be translated to difficulty; distress is another way of saying anxiety; famine is stating great lack; and then there is peril, which represents insecurity. Paul could not have been clearer. He was saying, "Listen, we will all at some point experience difficult times that cause anxiety. We may even face lack in some area of our lives that might be used as a weapon to cause us to be insecure. However, these issues do not negate or change the love God has for us, nor should it change our love for Him." At the end of it all, His love supersedes our wildest dreams, and it's not going anywhere. Our names are forever etched in the palms of His hands, greater than that He holds us in His heart.

"We will never find a greater love than this."

MARVELOUS

REVELATION 15:3-4 (KJV)

And they sing the song of Moses the servant of God, and the song of the Lamb, saying, Great and marvellous are thy works, Lord God Almighty; just and true are thy ways, thou King of saints. Who shall not fear thee, O Lord, and glorify thy name? for thou only art holy: for all nations shall come and worship before thee; for thy judgments are made manifest.

SINGING is one of the purest forms of communication and worship. Even David declared that we must enter into God's presence with thanksgiving and praise in *PSALMS 100:4.* Have you ever been in a hectic situation that when it came to a screeching halt, you belted out a quick tune that in your mind was a form of applause? I have on several occasions. However, I would like to give you an informative clue: sing in the midst of the storm; do your best not to wait 'til it ends. Paul and Syrus, when thrown in the dingy prison, sang, and the prison doors were immediately opened. The three Hebrew boys declared, as their form of praise, God would deliver them from the fiery furnace. All three came out without even the smell of smoke on their garments. The song of Moses celebrated Israel's deliverance from Egypt, when God parted the Red Sea *(EXODUS 15).* The song of the Lamb celebrates the ultimate deliverance of God's people from the power of Satan, showing God's judgment, power, and sovereignty. I am certain that it pleases God when we sing in the midst of a storm, simply because we are confident that God is not a respecter of any of His children. He will rescue each of us at His appointed time and place us back on dry, unheated ground.

"A song of praise gets me closer to my deliverance."

NATURALLY

JOHN 19:30 (NIV)

When he had received the drink, Jesus said, "It is finished." With that, he bowed his head and gave up his spirit.

MALLORY chose *natural:* Organic without process; free from constraint.

Naturally Forgiving
Naturally Loving
Naturally Wise
Naturally Unfailing
Naturally Longsuffering
Naturally Kind
Naturally Absolute
Naturally Infinite
Naturally Creative
Naturally Available
Naturally Intentional
Naturally Worthy
Naturally, He is Holy
Naturally, He is God

"Naturally gave His life for your life."

OMNIPRESENT

ISAIAH 57:15 (NASB)

For thus says the high and exalted One Who lives forever, whose name is Holy,
"I dwell on a high and holy place, And also with the contrite and lowly of spirit
In order to revive the spirit of the lowly
And to revive the heart of the contrite.

WE met in 1995, through a mutual friend over a Thanksgiving dinner. Quickly, we became sisters. When I sent my request regarding the letters of the alphabet, Edie's letter was *O*. The word she chose was *omnipresent.* I immediately had a revelation about the word she chose, but first I had a question to ask. "How long have you been saved?" Edie said, "Since 2003. I confessed Christ as my savior when I was 12, but didn't have a full understanding of what I was doing." Edie went further, telling me this, "It's actually a funny story. I was down south in Alabama with my grandmother, and she gave me a book marker that had the Lord's Prayer on it. I memorized the Lord's Prayer, and she made me and my cousin go lie in beds in our rooms for hours saying the Lord's Prayer over and over, asking the Lord to come into our hearts. Then I confessed Him as my Savior. I may have laid there for two or three hours doing this. I believe I was expecting some miracle or bright light or some special feeling, but nothing really happened. But I did learn the Lord's Prayer." I think what makes this childhood memory sweet is that what this little girl was expecting took place. He showed up in her midst. How do I know? *Omni* (all) *presence* (present), so God is present everywhere at all times with no exceptions. There is no place where we can go and He is not there. He is everywhere in all places always, which tells me He was there in Alabama while this little girl recited over and over the Lord's Prayer. He is omnipresent.

"Even the clouds do not obstruct His view."

PRISTINE PROMISE

Matthew 1:23 (NIV)

*"The virgin will conceive and give birth to a son,
and they will call him Immanuel"
(which means "God with us").*

Pristine; having its original purity, uncorrupted and immaculate. What a magnificent and appropriate word selected by my very dear friend, LaDonna! I can recall the two of us having a conversation where we posed this thought. Imagine, for just a moment, being the Savior's Mother, to be the one whom God chose as the vessel to bring Salvation to the earth. I'm reminded of a verse from a song that always makes me teary, "And when you kiss your little baby, you have kissed the face of God." The thought leaves me speechless, knowing my friend as well as I do, that of all the things in life that she has accomplished, she will tell you that being Ryan, Kyle, and Tyler's mother is her greatest. "Children are the purest of souls," she would often say, so I am not surprised that she chose a word such as *pristine* which, in essence, describes our Savior's innocent nature. *"For to us a child is born, to us a son is given, and the government will be on his shoulders. And he will be called Wonderful Counselor, Mighty God, Everlasting Father, Prince of Peace" (Isaiah 9:6).*

Wonderful Counselor:
He is exceptional, always giving us the correct directions.

Mighty God:
He is God alone.

Everlasting Father:
He is timeless, without an end.

Prince of Peace:
He reigns in justice and peace.

"This Child is our Deliverer."

QUINTESSENTIAL

JOHN 14:6 (KJV)

Jesus saith unto him, I am the way, the truth, and the life: no man cometh unto the Father, but by Me.

WITHOUT the air, we could not breathe. Without water, our bodies would shut down. Without Christ as Savior, we would die. *Quintessential* is defined in Webster's: "Of the pure and essential essence of something; the most perfect embodiment of what matters." *Quint* alone means king. *Essential* means absolutely necessary; indispensable. We are nothing without Christ, and we can do nothing without Him. We couldn't save ourselves, and we would have wanted to. We were dead in sin when Christ died for us and paid the price for us in full. Think about your life before He chose you. That's right, you did not choose Him, He chose you. Jesus made the first choice when He gave His life, deciding in that moment that He wanted us to live with Him forever and free from the bondage of slavery which was sin. I think it rather amazing that *quint* also means king. After all, He is the King of Kings and the Lord of Lords, which makes our need for Him essential. Jesus is quintessential. If heaven is your goal, accepting this quintessential Savior is absolutely necessary. Do not try to live without Him.

"Without exception, He is our only way."

REDEEMER

1 Timothy 1:14 (KJV)

And the grace of our Lord was exceeding abundant with faith and love which is in Christ Jesus.

The redemptive power of Christ has ensured that grace has made its way to each of us daily. I love music and today while on a long drive, I heard a song, and the lyrics simply said, "Grace made its way to me." Wow! The next verse, "I've been redeemed by the love of my father, redeemed by the hand of my Savior redeemed, lovingly saved. Grace made its way to me." Mercy triumphs over justice in this redemptive plan. While studying to write this devotion, I looked *Redeemer* up in the dictionary. There was only one line, and it read, "Jesus Christ." Not surprised that, while there are many to claim not to believe in Him, the dictionary made it plain. Jesus is our Redeemer, and our Redeemer lives.

"Redeemed by love and His Blood."

SAVIOR

MATTHEW 1:21 (NIV)

She will give birth to a son,
and you are to give him the name Jesus,
because he will save his people from their sins."

THE conception of Jesus was supernatural. It is beyond human logic or reasoning. God, knowing us as He does, needed to be certain that His careful plans would come fully to pass. He sent angels to deliver the news to Mary and Joseph. Angels are spiritual beings created by God to assist Him in work that needs to be accomplished on earth. Can you imagine the weight Joseph must have felt in those first few seconds? His wife, a virgin, was carrying the Savior of the world. The angel declared to Joseph that Mary was going to give birth to a son, which had been conceived by the Holy Spirit. This vast statement brings truth to light. Jesus is both God and human. The absolute, immeasurable Christ laid down His divinity to become human. He decided to be born to die for our sins. He and the Father calculated this redemptive plan. I'm speaking about the Savior, but I am also letting you know through this revelation that, just as God devised this plan for His Son, when we feel the unimaginable weight of the world on our shoulders, when quick decisions are required, try checking in with the One who incubated in the womb of a virgin for nine months on purpose. He did it all for your purposes to fully come to pass. His name is Jesus, which means "The Lord Saves."

"The Lord who saves is God with us."

TREMENDOUS

Psalms 145:7-9 (NLT)

Everyone will share the story of your wonderful goodness; they will sing with joy about your righteousness. The LORD is merciful and compassionate, slow to get angry and filled with unfailing love. The LORD is good to everyone. He showers compassion on all his creation.

Tremendous: extraordinarily great in size, amount, or intensity; extraordinary in excellence.

Mrs. Sandra Campbell, in her own words, wrote:

God's Love for me is Tremendous.

He keeps me. He protects me. He covers me.

He supplies my needs.

He surprises me with blessings beyond my imagination. He keeps my mind in perfect peace.

He keeps me in good health.

For my husband, my children, my grandbabies, my family, my friends, my Church, my love for God with all that He has done makes–it all *TREMENDOUS!* God is full of love. He satisfies all who trust Him. I can agree with Mrs. C, for all His goodness makes Him Tremendous.

"Tremendously blessed are those whose God is the Lord."

UNFAILING

UNFAILING ~ PSALMS 13:5 (NIV)

But I trust in your unfailing love; my heart rejoices in your salvation.

VINE ~ JOHN 15:5 (NIV)

I am the vine, you are the branches. If you remain in me, and I in you, you will bear much fruit; apart from me you can do nothing.

WORD ~ JOHN 1:1 (NIV)

In the beginning was the Word, and the Word was with God, and the Word was God.

eXAMPLE ~ JOHN 13:15-17 (NIV)

I have set you an example that you should do as I have done for you. Very truly I tell you, no servant is greater than his master, nor is a messenger greater than the one who sent him. Now that you know these things, you will be blessed if you do them.

YOKE ~ MATTHEW 11:29-30 (NIV)

Take my yoke upon you and learn from me, for I am gentle and humble in heart, and you will find rest for your souls. For my yoke is easy and my burden is light.

ZEAL ~ ROMANS 12:11 (NIV)

Never be lacking in zeal, but keep your spiritual fervor, serving the Lord.

"A to Z, the beginning and the end."

VICARIOUS

2 CORINTHIANS 5:21 (KJV)

For he hath made him to be sin for us, who knew no sin; that we might be made the righteousness of God in him.

DR. Donna Hunter chose *vicarious*—such an appropriate word to describe our God. *Vicarious* means to suffer in place of another; take an undeserved punishment. In your wildest dreams, can you imagine punishing your only child for the entire world? The action that took place at the cross could be considered "the Great Exchange." At our conversion, we exchanged our sin for His righteousness. At the cross, our sins were placed on Jesus. People make exchanges all the time. In most cases, it is always for equal value. However, God, through His Only Son, offered us the Great Exchange—something of immeasurable worth for something worthless. When God looked at you and me, He deemed us worthy, so He vicariously, through His Only Son, made atonement for us. Christ is the substitute for us. He was without sin. He became sin for us.

"For such a high priest became us, who is holy, harmless, undefiled, separate from sinners, and made higher than the heavens" (HEBREWS 7:26), we should be ever-so-grateful for His loving kindness toward us. We were useless in our state of sin, however, when the Great Exchange took place, our lives became priceless. Our price went up, no longer on sale for the enemy to possibly purchase at a reduced price. That's what sin does; it causes us to reduce our standards and become slaves to that thing that so easily besets us. However, when that "blood-purchased" tag is placed on us, our adversary shops elsewhere. He still stops by every now and again to see if we decided to go on clearance, but he quickly sees that the price has been marked up and that security is watching for any possible thieves. Our security is constant and is found only in Jesus Christ.

"The blood of Jesus Christ increased our value."

WONDERFUL

Psalms 119:129 (NASB)

Your testimonies are wonderful;
Therefore my soul observes them.

I gave a few of my friends a letter from the alphabet and asked them to give me a word that came to mind about our Lord. Willa, appropriately, had the letter *W*. She chose *wonderful. Wonderful* is another way of saying marvelous, amazing, and extraordinary. Having spent countless hours with her, I could clearly see why this is the first word that came to mind. Her testimony is astounding. Not growing up in the Church, she took a risk at learning who this big God was. She watched Him time and time again show His great big hand in her life, wonderful! She started her own publishing company and had more people sign with her than I am sure she could ever imagine, wonderful! It takes a brave heart to dare to trust a God that was new to her, wonderful! I guess in life, no matter what stage, once you know Him, you automatically love Him, and words such as *wonderful* come easily. He has proven Himself to be just that– wonderful. When you meet people for the first time, they have a story. When you meet the Creator, He proves Himself by His written Word that He puts above His name. That's wonderful!

"He is extraordinarily amazing and wonderful."

X~CELLENT

ISAIAH 12:5 (KJV)

Sing unto the LORD; for he hath done excellent things: this is known in all the earth.

EXCELLENT: possessing outstanding quality or superior merit; remarkably good. The sun is the star at the center of the solar system. It is a nearly perfect sphere of hot plasma with internal convective motion that generates a magnetic field via a dynamo process. It is by far the most important source of energy for life on earth. Jesus is our source for life. He is also known as the morning star. God's plans are excellent. Just as the sun is the center of the solar system, Christ desires to be the center of our lives. This scripture from Isaiah speaks of the excellent things God has done. Clearly, Jesus is the greatest gift God has given us. This excellent Christ is worthy of the highest praise. Glance at nature's canvas: the massive blue sky, the Blood Falls in Antarctica, the rainbow eucalyptus trees in Hawaii, the light pillars over Moscow, the Northern Lights, Mount Everest, Iguazu Falls, and then there is the Great Barrier Reef, just to name a few of God's creative excellences at work. However, in his letter to the Ephesians, Paul tells us *we* are God's work of art, His greatest masterpiece in all of creation. Our salvation is something only God can do. It is His excellent powerful creative work in us through Christ.

"The Master has His greatest work in his hands."

YOU'RE AMAZING

PSALMS 47:2 (NIV)

For the LORD Most High is awesome,
the great King over all the earth.

You positioned Yourself to give us Salvation, You're **Amazing.**

You gave Your only begotten Son, You're **Amazing.**

You are Jesus, who died for us while we were still sinners, You're **Amazing.**

We are forgiven for past, present, and future sins, You're **Amazing.**

Your mercies are new every morning, You're **Amazing.**

You created the heavens and the earth, You're **Amazing.**

Your grace is sufficient for all our trials, You're **Amazing.**

Of all Your creations, we are Your greatest masterpiece, You're **Amazing.**

Your plans for us are all good, You're **Amazing.**

You're omnipresent, omniscient, and omnipotent, You're **Amazing.**

Your Kingdom will never end, You're **Amazing.**

You're **Amazing.**

You promised to never leave us or forsake us, You're **Amazing.**

Your Word is above Your Name, that's **Amazing.**

"You are the King of Glory. You're Amazing!"

Z

REVELATION 21:6 (HCSB)

And He said to me, "It is done! I am the Alpha and the Omega, the Beginning and the End. I will give water as a gift to the thirsty from the spring of life."

Z, THE last letter in the alphabet, means God has the final say in our lives. He is the Judge. He is the Alpha and Omega, who declares He is the beginning and the end. There is no one besides His Son and His Spirit. There is no other Bread of Life. God completed His original plan in creation that was remarkably great. Christ completed His work in our ransom. The Trinity will complete its salvation when all the redeemed join Him in glory. When I think of God being the first and the last, I equate it to the following attributes, which all end with Him:

Everlasting to everlasting–*Thou art God.*
Bountiful–*His storehouse is full.*
He is Unequaled–*He cannot be surpassed.*
Unparalleled–*He is peerless.*
Steadfast–*He never changes.*
Without Limits–*"He is not constrained or inhibited."*

"He is beyond compare, He is matchless in every way."

TWO WILL DO

Deuteronomy 32:30 (KJV)

How should one chase a thousand, and two put ten thousand to flight, except their Rock had sold them, and the Lord had shut them up?

I was at the park getting my workout in for the day, when suddenly my phone sent me an alert, so I stopped a brief moment to check. I was certain that the nudge I felt in my spirit was divinely orchestrated by the Holy Spirit because I was so engrossed in checking my phone; the last thing on my mind was to look down at my feet. It was just then I noticed there was a snake just inches from my ankle. Yikes! First, I screamed, and then I ran only to see that my reaction caused the creepy crawler to literally leap from the ground in a panic and slither back into the bush from which it came. Needless to say, I couldn't get out of the park fast enough and I vowed to my own self never to walk in this park again. Every hair on my body stood at full attention; every goose bump there ever was I was confidently sporting.

When I got back to *mi casa,* I texted my best friend, Gena. She quickly replied, "The devil is a liar." However, it was Gena's second response that really made me think of that moment as a spiritual encounter. "He was just as afraid of you as you were of him." Wow! Because of whose I am and because I am covered in the blood, he couldn't touch me with his venomous bite.

Early the next day, Gena called to ask if I would like to join her on her morning stroll at the park. I said, "Yes, but not the park where I walked yesterday." Quick to give me another lesson, she replied, "I am not scared of no snakes." So, I loaded up the car with cold water, my iPod, and rollerblades. Yep, forget walking or running—I will skate, a quicker getaway. When I arrived at the park to meet my courageous-around-reptiles buddy, she again added another teaching moment to our workout journey. She spoke the same words as Moses spoke to the Israelites. "How could one chase a thousand, and two put ten thousand to flight, unless their Rock had sold them, and the Lord had shut them up?" This was a moment of revelation. First, the snake could not harm me unless God said it was okay, and second, because I adhered to the prompting of the Holy Spirit. He kept me safe. Yes, *two will do,* however, the Divine Trinity will be there, too.

"Holy Spirit, go before me with every step I take.
I know Your promise is to keep me safe."

AUTHOR

PSALM 48:14 (KJV)

For this God is our God forever and ever: he will be our guide even unto death.

AUTHOR OF ETERNAL SALVATION ~ HEBREWS 5:9 (KJV)

And having been perfected,
He became the author of eternal salvation to all who obey Him.

BUCKLER ~ PROVERBS 2:7 (KJV)

He layeth up sound wisdom for the righteous:
he is a buckler to them that walk uprightly.

CHRIST THE LORD ~ LUKE 2:11 (KJV)

For unto you are born this day in the city of David a Saviour,
which is Christ the Lord.

DOOR ~ JOHN 10:7 (KJV)

Then said Jesus unto them again, verily, verily, I say unto you,
I am the door of the sheep.

EXCELLENT ~ PSALMS 148:13 (KJV)

Let them praise the name of the LORD: for his name alone is excellent;
his glory is above the earth and heaven.

JEALOUS

Foundation ~ 1 Corinthians 3:11 (KJV)

For other foundation can no man lay than that is laid, which is Jesus Christ.

Governor ~ Psalms 22:28 (KJV)

For the kingdom is the Lord's: and he is the governor among the nations.

Husband ~ Isaiah 54:5 (KJV)

For thy Maker is thine husband; the Lord of hosts is his name;
and thy Redeemer the Holy One of Israel;
The God of the whole earth shall he be called.

Intercessor ~ Romans 8:26 (KJV)

Likewise the Spirit also helpeth our infirmities:
for we know not what we should pray for as we ought:
but the Spirit itself maketh intercession for us with
groanings which cannot be uttered.

Jealous ~ Exodus 34:14 (KJV)

For thou shalt worship no other god: for the Lord,
whose name is Jealous, is a jealous God

King of Kings ~ 1 Timothy 1:17 (KJV)

Now unto the King eternal, immortal, invisible, the only wise God,
be honour and glory forever and ever. Amen.

Life ~ John 14:6 (KJV)

Jesus saith unto him, I am the way, the truth, and the life:
no man cometh unto the Father, but by me.

Messiah ~ John 14:6 (KJV)

The woman saith unto Him, I know that Messiah cometh, which is called Christ:
when he is come, he will tell us all things.
Jesus saith unto her, I that speak unto thee am he.

A TEACHER, TOO

NAZARENE ~ MATTHEW 2:23 (KJV)

And he came and dwelt in a city called Nazareth:
that it might be fulfilled which was spoken by the prophets,
He shall be called a Nazarene.

OMEGA ~ REVELATION 22:13 (KJV)

I am Alpha and Omega, the beginning and the end, the first and the last.

POTTER ~ ISAIAH 64:8 (KJV)

But now, O Lord, thou art our father; we are the clay, and thou our potter;
and we all are the work of thy hand.

QUICKENING SPIRIT ~ 1 CORINTHIANS 15:45 (KJV)

And so it is written, The first man Adam was made a living soul;
the last Adam was made a quickening spirit.

REWARDER ~ HEBREWS 11:6 (KJV)

But without faith it is impossible to please him: for he that cometh to God must believe that he is, and that he is a rewarder of them that diligently seek him.

SALVATION ~ SONG ~ STRENGTH ~ ISAIAH 12:2 (KJV)

Behold, God is my salvation; I will trust, and not be afraid:
for the Lord Jehovah is my strength and my song;
he also is become my salvation.

TEACHER ~ JOHN 13:13 (KJV)

Ye call me Master and Lord: and ye say well; for so I am.

BOTTLED UP

PSALMS 56:8 (KJV, MSG)

Thou tellest my wanderings: put thou my tears into thy bottle:
are they not in thy book?
You've kept track of my every toss and turn through the sleepless nights,
each tear entered in your ledger, each ache written in your book.

WE have all had a day, a week, a month and, for some, we have even had seasons where the best we could do was muster up tears to release some of the bottled-up emotions of who we are, or better yet, what we are faced with. The best reasonable response was our very own tears. Well, I have great news for those who have had these types of seasons. Our tears were not wasted on Kleenex. Better than that, the Master has collected them all. The greater news is this, along with our bottled tears that the Father collected, was a ledger written that listed what caused the aches that caused the tears. Amazing! Every tear has mattered, none of them wasted. Like a baby's mother knows the different cries of her child—hungry, wet, tired, sick, or just needing a little TLC—our Father has an ear to understanding our every tear that we have ever cried. *"Those that sow in tears shall reap in joy." (PSALMS 126:5, KJV)*

"Our tears are priceless. That's why they have been bottled by the Master."

BRAND NEW

MATTHEW 9:17 (NKJV)

Nor do they put new wine into old wineskins, or else the wineskins break, the wine is spilled, and the wineskins are ruined. But they put new wine into new wineskins, and both are preserved.

I WAS the kid growing up that really did not fit in just any group or clique. It was as though I was always the odd man out. I remember a few times even trying to pretend that I was just like the other kids just so that I could be included; I was always found out. Sneaky was not something I was ever good at. I always got caught. In biblical days, wine was not kept in a bottle but in goatskins sewn around the edges to form watertight bags. New wine would expand as it fermented, stretching its wineskin. After the wine had aged, the stretched skin would burst if more wine were poured into it. Jesus did not come to patch up the old religious systems with their rules and traditions. If He had, this message we read today would have been damaged. The purpose of Christ's existence was to bring us something new, not tainted or polished by man's vine- yard. This new message declares that Jesus Christ, God's only begotten Son, came to offer reconciliation and forgiveness to all men. Just as the old wine could not be poured into new wineskins, this glorious gospel would not fit in with the old legalistic system known as religion. God's message will always remain *new* because it must be accepted and applied in every generation.

Ferment: inflame; foment. **Inflame:** to be kindled with passion. **Foment:** to promote growth and development.

I believe it safe to say that our Lord and Savior came kindled with passion to promote His Father's written Word for our growth, development, and salvation.

"Yes, He has made us brand New."

RELUCTANT EDITH

GENESIS 19:26 (ESV)

*But Lot's wife, behind him, looked back,
and she became a pillar of salt.*

RELUCTANT Edith, that was Lot's wife. What was her hesitancy? What transpired in her life in Sodom that made it difficult for her to follow the instructions of her husband, who had clear instructions from the two angels that God sent to destroy the entire city, even its nearest plains? We must spend time at the Father's feet, so when He speaks, we know it's Him speaking. God favors those who, like Lot, have integrity and obedience. Oftentimes, the instructions the Lord gives us are bigger than us. They seem outlandish. The truth is, that's how we know it's God. Be careful who you share your directives with. They may laugh, just like Lot's sons-in-law. This laughter was designed to stop you from fulfilling the plans God designed for you. These plans were carefully set in motion with you in mind. They are to prosper you, keep harm from you, bring love to you, and bring success to you. Therefore, I have two suggestions: stop looking back, the past is the past; and keep close to your heart your plans, because everyone you tell may not always be for you. Jesus said that we are the salt of the earth. Perhaps Edith was turned into a pillar of salt because in her death she became what she should have been while living.

"Disobedience and talking too much have heavy consequences."

EVERYTHING

Philippians 4:19 (KJV)

But my God shall supply all your need according to his riches in glory by Christ Jesus.

God has given us *"all things that pertain unto life and godliness."* By his *"exceeding great and precious promises,"* he has made it possible for us to *"be partakers of the divine nature"* *(2 Peter 1:3-4).* I shall not try, in this paper, to collect all the promises that God has given to those who believe in His Son, Jesus Christ. They are many, and they are *"exceeding great and precious."* My purpose is simply to show that if we live up to the conditions He has expressed or implied, *faithful* is the Lord of all. He promised to supply all our needs, not a few but all. I looked closer at this promise, and as I did, I came across the well-known scripture *Psalm 23:1, "The Lord is my shepherd; I shall not want."* Then I found myself peering at *Psalm 68:5, "a father of the fatherless, and a Judge of the widows, is god in his holy habitation."*

Paul and David had clear revelation of the father supplying all of their needs. David spent his early days before he was king as a shepherd, so he understood that the sheep depended on him for all their needs. Sheep are completely dependent on the shepherd for provision, guidance, and protection. Paul, in spite of all the troubles he had faced, desired to love and obey the Lord Jesus Christ with contentment. Wow! Like Paul and David, we must be content in knowing that, "Father knows best." Sometimes our wants do not line up with God's big plan, however, trusting in Christ by following His lead, our attitudes and appetites will change from wanting everything to accepting His provisional plans. We can trust that God will always meet our needs. Whatever we need on earth, He shall provide. He said everything; I trust He means everything you should too.

"The God whose kingdom will never end He is everything."

FOREVER

PSALMS 29:10-11 (NKJV)

The Lord sat enthroned at the Flood,
And the Lord sits as King forever.
The Lord will give strength to His people;
The Lord will bless His people with peace.

NOTICE the psalmist said *forever.* The choice of words is pivotal to our great God. *Forever* denotes eternal, endless, perpetual, permanent, always, and for keeps. Furthermore, he expresses with certainty that the heavenly Father also promises to give strength to us as His children then solidifies this pledge with the precious gift of peace. Forever the Lord of Glory shall stand as Lord of all. His is the kingdom that shall never end. Jesus Christ His Son will forever be seated at His right hand. I remember growing up with my grandmother and one day, while she was making my favorite PB&J sandwich, she blurted out, "TeeCee, you know I am not going be here forever." What? Why? MeeMaw promptly explained then that nothing lasts forever. I recall running down the hall to my room to get in my secret place, the closet. After a few moments of sobbing, I heard her outside my closet door, whispering to come out so we could talk amidst my tears and the aroma from the PB&J. I found myself in her arms in my green room on my twin bed. MeeMaw said, "Nothing lasts forever. No, not one thing." I must inform you that I was about six or seven years of age at the time, so she spoke in a language I could grasp. Elementary! She reminded me of the lessons I had recently learned at St. Albert's Catholic school in my catechism classes. In catechism, we were taught about how Jesus died but rose on the third day, and because He died for us, when we leave this earth, we will be with Him in heaven. Still a little limited in my understanding, I let it go, but only for a while. Therefore, at least once a week she had to hear me say, "How are you feeling today?" I was able to share 18 more years with MeeMaw before she went home to be with our Lord. In those 18 years, I learned many life lessons that I will forever hold close to my heart. We are the lives He gave His life for. We are His guests. He is forever our invitation. Our Father is the Living Word that shall never cease. Every written promise shall *forever* endure.

"God Eternal created us for Him to love forever."

HAVE CONFIDENCE

1 John 5:14 (ESV)

And this is the confidence that we have toward him, that if we ask anything according to his will he hears us.

The weight of this passage is bundled carefully with explicit in- structions as to how to get your prayers answered and at the same time please God because we followed His absolute directions. When we pray, we should never demand to have our own way, but rather we ask Him what He wants for us. If we coordinate our wants with His desires for us, He will listen, and He will answer giving us the definite resolution to the now clear picture ahead. When life hits you blindsided, you are already in frenzy. Why add more to your dilemma? Since He has your name written in the palms of His hands, we should have confidence that His word is true, and He is sitting patiently to get involved in our circumstance: the good ones, the indifferent, and even the bad. Start by praying with confidence. This pleases the Father and shows Him you trust Him.

"Confidence is trust turned up."

HOPE & WAIT

ISAIAH 40:31 (GW)

Yet, the strength of those who wait with hope in the Lord will be renewed. They will soar on wings like eagles. They will run and won't become weary. They will walk and won't grow tired.

Hope: the feeling that what is wanted can be had or that events will turn out for the best

Wait: to remain inactive or in a state of repose, as until something expected happens

THERE is a general principle here that patient, praying believers are blessed by God when we wait in hope that He will deliver us from our trials. The word *hope* implies both trust and patience.Trust involves confidence in God's unwavering power to keep His promise to us regardless of what we are facing. We have all faced some sort of storm that feels like it would never end. Well, understand this: God's timing is not our timing. God does not deal in time but out of time. Ouch! Right here is the most critical part of the hoping and waiting. God knows exactly how long the storm will last and just how long we need to be in it for Him to get His perfected result from our life. David declared in *PSALMS 28:7* that the joy of the Lord was his strength, therefore, because we trusted Him God helped, and when He did, it caused David to rejoice in song. Paul said to the Corinthian church that it is the spirit of God that searches the spirit in us to make known the mysteries of God, to reveal to us the wisdom we will need to hope and wait. For we must know that truly we face some trials about which our human intellect could not gather the proper insight to stand, hope, and wait.

"Waiting on God's timing He is never late"

OUR GIFTS MAKE ROOM

Proverbs 18:16 (ESV)

A man's gift makes room for him
and brings him before the great.

So, here we all come together to celebrate a moment of achievement. The occasion? The completion of three years of ministry school. Caps and gowns, flowers, smiles, and a few tears that simply state, "We did it." Among the graduates, at some point we all wanted to quit, but we did not. We stayed our course and now are among an elite group called Finishers. This accomplishment comes with a few detailed yet very important kingdom assignments. They are certified, licensed, and some ordained. My name is called. I make my way to the podium. In this moment, I see these words come alive, "God anointed, man appointed." My Pastors Dr. Fred Hodge and Linda G. Hodge anoint and pray over me then declare before God and man I am a licensed, ordained minister. Tears and more tears. I am humbled yet again that the Master chose me to do bidding on the earth on His behalf. To seal the acts of this moment and to alleviate any doubt I may have, I received a call a few hours later from a very close friend requesting that I marry her daughter and fiancé in a few months. I concede but not before I thank the Lord of all for allowing me to see this Word come alive...your gift will make room for you.

"There is always room for your gift."

SACRED CONNECTION

1 SAMUEL 18:3 (NIV)

And Jonathan made a covenant with David because he loved him as himself.

To grasp the power and importance of our human connections is pivotal to where we must go, as well as where we have already been. If you think about it, there was someone in your past that lined you up for this very moment. Jonathan and David's lives yield an amazing story about loyalty, self-worth, and friendship, as well as love, honor, and at the end of it all, respect. If you know the story, you will understand that Jonathan was Saul's son, and because of Saul's heart for David, Jonathan, the prince, would not inherit the kingdom. Can you imagine walking with the one who, in time, would take your place? Because he was a devout worshiper, Jonathan recognized early on that David was to be anointed the King of Israel. Therefore, he willingly offered his robe of succession to David, his friend.

Some may ask how Jonathan could do it. The answer is this Sacred Connection far exceeds our imagination. Are you aware of your Sacred Connections? Both Jonathan and David remained faithful to God in their relationship, and for this reason they were able to handle what was to come. As the story ends, we learn neither Jonathan nor David allowed their flesh to rise and get in the way of what God wanted them to do. Our Father in heaven has allowed us to connect with someone, somewhere for such a time as this. Jonathan and David were confident in the Father, their loyalty to one another and obedience to the Father, made this Sacred Connection work. We must understand that God honors loyalty, obedience, faithfulness, and love. I often tell the Father, "Thank you for my human connections." While He alone is my spiritual source, my human connections often lend me a natural push to get me to take my next step.

"God, before the foundations, chose Jesus as our Sacred Connection."

LIBERATE YOURSELF

PHILIPPIANS 4:6-7 (NKJV)

*Be anxious for nothing, but in everything by prayer and supplication,
with thanksgiving, let your requests be made known to God;
And the peace of God, which surpasses all understanding,
will guard your hearts and minds through Christ Jesus.*

WHO'S anxious? Life is happening at the speed of light. The doctor delivers the news your son needs brain surgery after being told five years earlier brain surgery was not an option. Your daughter decides to move to another state. Imagine never being anxious about anything. What would our minds do if we did not worry? I don't have the answer exactly, but according to the scripture listed above, that would be a wise place to start. I choose peace over anxiety any day. Paul emphasizes here with a great deal of compassion that anxiety is a definite form of our inability to sit back and just believe that, in the end, God really will let it work out in our favor and ultimately for His good.

At the end of any day, it is not our weeping moments that attract God's attention. When surprising occasions present themselves, our first reaction should be not to allow our thoughts to make us anxious or to panic as if God forgot about us, but in fact, let our reactions be those of one walking in a stature of faith by prayer and supplication. *"With thanksgiving, let your requests be made known to God; And the peace of God, which surpasses all understanding, will guard your hearts and minds through Christ Jesus."*

"Choose peace over panic."

WELL DONE

Psalm 30:5 (ISV)

For his wrath is only momentary;
yet his favor is for a lifetime. Weeping may lodge for the night,
but shouts of joy will come in the morning.

When we know Him and we look closely at the cross, we should understand the suffering He endured, not physically, but emotionally. For Christ had the cross experience for you and me. The crown, the scourging, the spitting, the name calling, the nails, even forgiving the one who hung there next to Him, it was all for us. When someone leaves us here on earth, our humanness wants them to stay, not fully considering the suffering they may have endured on the journey to their final rest. Look at Peter when Christ explained that He was going to leave. Jesus rebuked him, because Jesus knew this was part of the plan. When someone dies, it's never a surprise to the Father. Scripture declares that to be absent from the body is to be present with the Lord *(2 Corinthians 5:8)*. Our natural loss is God's great reward that we finally come back home.

While we know we will miss our sister, we are grateful her painful days are no more. LaVonne was an Amazing sister. The love of Christ preceded her very being. The Father knew He could trust her with all she endured, and He also knew it would essentially bring her right near to Him. Weeping may endure for the night, but joy comes in the morning. When LaVonne arrived at heaven's gates, there was no more weeping, no more suffering, no more tears. I can clearly hear my sister say, "I made it, and I'm glad to be home." And with that, the Father smiled and said, "You have finished your course and won your race. *WELL DONE, MY GOOD AND FAITHFUL SERVANT, LAVONNE!*"

For Diva Tami Wilburn, an amazing sister and friend.

WHEN IT MAKES NO SENSE

PHILIPPIANS 4:7 (ESV)

And the peace of God, which surpasses all understanding, will guard your hearts and your minds in Christ Jesus.

I WAS talking to my brother-in-law a week after losing his mother, my mother-in-law. Don explained to me that while he has his moments, for the most part he's at peace. The initial call simply hurt so badly, it felt unreal. I have been a part of this family 31 years. She was my mom, too. My mother-in-law gave birth to four children, one of whom preceded her in death. Therefore, I'm certain she had fully experienced true love and, with this loss of her first child, she also knew true pain and grief. As I sat there that night, he explained all the different emotions he had experienced, the ones before her passing and now his present ones. How does one explain that, yes, it hurts deeply, but also it is well with one's soul? As we sat there discussing our loss, I heard the Comforter say to me, "When you walk with me, there is a peace that surpasses all understanding. I put on you the peace I have about my love for you. Nothing in the world that I created can change the loving peace I have towards you. *NOTHING!*"

Don even expressed to me that he believed Ms. Elvera, Gran-El as we children affectionately called her, at that time she, too, had a peace. As I write this today, I'm reminded that even in times of distress for Jesus Christ, He always seemed to find a peace that would allow Him to complete the journey He and His Father authored. Even in the beginning, the middle, and the end, when we begin to say, "This makes no sense," we will suddenly be reminded that we have His peace that surpasses all understanding. We can then continue our journey that our loved ones would want us to complete, because we all have a purpose and a destiny, and to stop living among the living would simply make no sense. I am grateful for that conversation with my brother-in-law Don, because I was able to gather this revelation. Peace, and be still.

"This peace I have makes it all well in my soul."

BULLY

1 Peter 5:8 (ISV)

Be clear-minded and alert. Your opponent, the devil, is prowling around like a roaring lion, looking for someone to devour.

He is the accuser of the brethren. Satan is that kid at school who punks the underdog, you know, the one who tries to intimidate the kids who look as though they are defeated, heads hung low, with a humdrum attitude. They mumble under their breath when you simply say, "Hello." Our courage is necessary daily; our armor is needed for this bully. The armor is our spiritual body gear that covers us from head to toe. We know the enemy plays dirty, so we must never leave home without suiting up in our combat gear daily.

I remember hearing my sister Myasha say, "Evil smells fear." What a profound statement. *1 Peter 5:8* makes it clear that our adversary, the devil (bully), is walking around seeking whom he can devour (punk). In that same verse, it paints a visual of how he's walking around. He is depicted as a ferocious animal—in this case, it is the lion. Lions attack stragglers, those who appear weak, often found alone and not alert. Evil smells fear. So, I suggest you start sitting at the Father's feet so He can expose you to yourself. I promise, He will show you that you are stronger than you think. He is your strength in times of weakness, and He is the goodness and mercy that follows us all our living days. He will show you that He is our refuge in times of trouble, that you are bolder than this fake lion. Popeye ate spinach, Superman goes into the phone booth, and Wonder Woman rips off her girly attire. These superheroes rush to aid the underdog. Jesus is our superhero. He gave His life for our sins, defeated our adversary, that fake ferocious animal, at the cross. Therefore, when this bully starts taunting or attempting to punk you, boldly look in his face and simply say, "Christ died for such a time as this. This territory is covered by His Blood; bullies are not welcome here."

"No trespassing: all bullies will be prosecuted to the full extent of the law."

ALWAYS ON TIME

JEREMIAH 29:11 (NIV)

"...For I know the plans I have for you," declares the Lord, "plans to prosper you and not to harm you, plans to give you hope and a future."

AMAZING is just one of the few small words I use to describe such a great big God. Disagreements, financial setbacks, divorce, moving after 12 long years (*foreclosure* is the proper term), empty nest syndrome on the horizon, Lord, can I buy a break? From comfortable quarters where we each had our own space to escape when necessary, to no room to essentially breathe, God, what lessons do I learn from this? What weapons do I use for this fight? Is this my test for my faith to grow? If so, will I pass? The season seemed forever. It became less stressful and easier to bear when I was reminded by my spirit of the words spoken by Jeremiah, that my life plans are in the Master's hand, and they are all good. Once I calmed down and took this written promise to heart, I could see that, yes, the plans were good, and they were on purpose for bigger reasons than I, in the heat of the moment, could understand. Therefore, I lean back and thank the Father that, because He holds my life in His hands, I trust that these plans will take me on a journey that He personally planned. I suggest you do the same the next time life throws you a curveball and you weren't wearing your glove. Trust and believe you will still win the game, the game called life. These plans are always on time.

"Glad to be a part of His plans."

WE ARE

Ephesians 2:10 (NLT)

For we are God's masterpiece. He has created us anew in Christ Jesus, so we can do the good things he planned for us long ago.

We are spiritually alive and free—No longer a slave to sin

We are citizens of heaven—Heaven is our permanent home

We are God's disciples—Ambassadors of Christ

We are the salt of the earth—Preserving lives as a witness

I think it is important every now and again to remind ourselves who we are in Christ. Oftentimes, we find our thoughts focusing on the negative things people have said about us or to us. Our lives are so important. . .we must cast down the negative chatter, only to realize who *We Are* in Christ. Imagine a day in your life when you rehearsed lines that read like this:

We are secure in Christ—Accepted completely by God

We are a place where God's Spirit lives—Temple of the Holy Ghost

We are God's incredible work of art—We are His greatest masterpiece

We are totally and completely forgiven—Transformed by the Blood

We are created In God's likeness—We have His DNA

We are the light of the world—Light shining before all men

We are greatly loved—Created for God to love

We have the mind of Christ—We do not have to be an emotional mess

"God created us to live an abundant life full of joy."

ANTI-THEFT

MATTHEW 6:14-15 (NKJV)

"For if you forgive men their trespasses,
your heavenly Father will also forgive you.
But if you do not forgive men their trespasses,
neither will your Father forgive your trespasses."

THE Holy Spirit offered this revelation during our Winner's Circle, a weekly book club formed by my pastor as a class designed to help heal, restore, and recover the broken pieces of our past.

This session, we are reviewing the book, *Let It Go*. Forgiveness is the "big idea" written in the pages of this book. Many would agree that, of all the laws set by our gracious Lord, forgiveness is the toughest of them all. The understanding I have come to is that, like most, we feel forgiveness is like letting the offender free. The true tactic to this big idea is to understand that, in fact, you are allowing yourself to get free. Forgiveness is not an emotion, but rather a deliberate movement of our will, a free choice to waive the entitlement owed by the wrongdoer.

As the night ended, a few ladies were still challenged with how this big idea would help them stop holding their offenders hostage. Leaving the class that night, a few of us hung out in the parking lot chatting, just as girls sometimes do. While we hung around talking, I asked to speak to one of the ministers, who quickly replied, "I don't know what is wrong with my car. When I unlock it, if I don't get in immediately, it locks itself." Another lady and I standing by shouted in unison, "Anti-theft!" and we exploded in laughter. However, it was the next moment that sealed the deal with this big idea. I felt a nudge in my spirit then expeditiously felt the need to share this new revelation about the big idea. Forgiveness is our anti-theft! Tears of joy filled our eyes with this breaking news about the big idea. Taking it a step further, I explained that most often, the light that indicates an anti-theft device in most vehicles typically flashed the color red. The common thief would pass this vehicle by and move to the next. I am reminded that just like when Pharaoh's army saw the blood on the doors, those homes were passed over. When Satan sees the blood on our lives, he may try to tamper just a bit, but eventually, he passes on to the next, where he sees no blood. Be sure to activate your anti-theft. It holds the forgiving power.

"Be quick to forgive and you stay forgiven."

I'M A BELIEVER

Psalms 103:21 (NIV)

Praise the Lord,
all his Heavenly hosts,
you his servants who do His will.

God requires us as believers to be restored and healed in all areas of brokenness. When this happens, God becomes our comforter, who enables us to function in a healthy and effective manner. This edifies the Body of Christ. When this transformation takes place, believers are in turn equipped to help those who have not established a relationship with Him. Believers are God's ambassadors. We should not be prideful or self-serving, but helpers (servants) who infuse joy. For believers to accomplish this great task, we must remember to utilize the essentials taught in the Word. Five ambassador prerequisites:

A **Comforter:** Support one another seeing deep into the heart of the matter, then ease this discomfort with the assistance of the Holy Ghost. *(Romans 15:4)*

Charitable: Show mercy and compassion, just as God extends to us daily. *(Amos 5:15)*

A **Good Listener:** Listen to the people just as they expect God to listen when we speak to Him. *(James 1:9)*

Meek: Meekness is a strength that has patience under control and is not easily moved to anger. God honors such character. *"Be completely humble and gentle; be patient, bearing with one another in love." (Ephesians 4:2)*

Humble: Be mindful that we are all God's children. He's not a respecter of persons, neither should we be. *"But the meek will inherit the land, and enjoy peace and prosperity." (Psalms 37:11)* Are you a believer?

"Good believers follow these principles."

CALCULATED PURPOSE

JOB 42:2 (ESV)

I know that you can do all things,
and that no purpose of yours can be thwarted.

Calculated: carefully thought out or planned

Purpose: (1) The reason for which something exists or is done, made, used, etc. (2) An intended or desired result; end; aim; goal. (3) Determination; resoluteness.

HIS PURPOSE IN OUR SALVATION

2 TIMOTHY 1:9 "who saved us and called us to a holy calling, not because of our works but because of his own purpose and grace, which He gave us in Christ Jesus before the ages began."

NOT YOUR PLANS BUT HIS PURPOSE

PROVERBS 19:21 "Many are the plans in the mind of a man, but it is the purpose of the LORD that will stand."

CANNOT BE VOIDED

ISAIAH 55:11 "so shall my word be that goes out from my mouth; it shall not return to me empty, but it shall accomplish that which I purpose, and shall succeed in the thing for which I sent it."

CALLED FOR HIS PURPOSE

ROMANS 8:28 "And we know that for those who love God all things work together for good, for those who are called according to his purpose."

"Strategically calculated are all His purposes."

HIS BIG IDEA

Ephesians 4:32 (NIV)

Be kind and compassionate to one another, forgiving each other just as in Christ God forgave you.

Forgiveness has the power to release your anointing.

Forgiveness is liberating; it helps us abandon our insecurities.

Forgiveness is a requirement from the Father.

Forgiveness gives us life back.

Forgiveness keeps us forgiven *(Luke 6:37) "Forgive, and you will be forgiven."*

Forgiveness teaches us mercy, the compassion of Christ.

Forgiveness helps us to keep this Commandment. *(Exodus 20:3) "You shall have no other gods before me."* Unforgiveness becomes a god, a grudge that is worshipped.

Rehearsing the offense magnifies the breach instead of magnifying the Father.

My willingness to forgive allows God to deal with my offender.

When we begin to practice the art of forgiveness, it becomes second nature to us. We will remember that we are not wrestling with flesh and blood but the rulers in the dark places who use our offender to attempt to cause us harm.

We often try to forgive people, but forgiveness can't do its redemptive work because we won't let it go. Holding on to this past offense reopens the wound, giving way to the senseless mind chatter, which breeds anger, and anger turns into unforgiveness.

"Forgiveness is God's BIG IDEA."

FAITH ~ HOPE ~ FEAR

Hebrews 11:1 (KJ21)

Now faith is the substance of things hoped for, the evidence of things not seen.

Here we are again. It is a cool January evening, and I am home alone. Jaylon and Chelsea are at work. I hear the garage door go up. Someone's home. Jaylon makes his way to my bedroom door, then utters these words, "Mom, do not panic." When you hear these words, what do you automatically do? Panic of course. Jay began to explain that he has already called his dad and that he will meet us at the hospital. Jay blurts out without blinking, "My right side is numb again." In this very moment I experience faith, hope, and the biggest of them all, fear. I thought we had finished this fight six years ago. In utter disbelief, I hear the doctors in the ER say words I was not ready to hear. Jay's brain has another bleeder. He will need to have brain surgery. Yes, I am a believer, but I am also Jaylon's mother. Faith is a daily test, in my opinion. I believe it depends on what the matters are. I don't cancel my faith in God, however, it is our initial reaction to many circumstances. When I come to my senses, I quickly convert my thinking pattern, based on my experience with the Father who has never failed me yet. Like David wrote, I will put my hope in the One who has an unfailing love for me. In these trembling times, I focus on this unfailing love, because God loves me completely, He shields me with His righteous hand. My faith is found in His hope. It is in the evidence of what I cannot see. When I allow this to be my guide over my thoughts, fear takes a backseat, and I witness another supernaturally answered prayer. The God I serve created the heavens and the earth from nothing but His words. Therefore, when He made the promise through Jesus' blood that we are healed, I stand sure and certain that, though I can't see the end, I know He does, so I hope.

"Elevate your faith & hope. Release your fears."

PRAY, DANCE, AND JAB

DEUTERONOMY 20:4 (HCSB)

For the LORD your God is the One who goes with you to fight for you against your enemies to give you victory.

OFTENTIMES, we must remind ourselves that whenever we are facing what appears to be an uphill battle, we have the Master right there beside us. The struggle, if we are honest, is that in most cases we do not allow our minds to focus on that one truth. Instead, we instantly panic.

The day is here, March 11, 2015, Jaylon's brain surgery. East Coast family has arrived, Church family along with my pastors are present, Chelsea, Ron, and of course my good friends come with snacks in tow. It's going to be a long day. Surgery is scheduled to take five hours. When we hit the seventh hour, and I am reminded that in times like these it is time to pray, dance, and jab—to pray and fight at the same time.

By the ninth hour, I recall that while there is a room full of people to support us, the One I've been praying to is here also. In this case, my enemy is my mind. I find myself vacillating from worst-case scenarios to making my body physically ill. I must recall that the last time we faced a difficult challenge, it was the Lord who brought us out and delivered to us a victory. Surely, He's going to do it again. "Theresa, just keep praying, dancing, and jabbing."

During a battle, the last thing you do is put down your weapon. My weapon is prayer. My dancing distracts my enemy. He is unaware that internally, I'm a mother in panic. I am not going to speak negatively in this atmosphere, so he has no clue. And lastly, I keep fighting with my strong jabs. God is the great physician. He loves Jaylon more than I ever could. He knew Jaylon before He trusted me to be his mother. Recognizing my human limitations and allowing God's strength to work through my fears and weaknesses, this great God we serve starts every battle from a place of victory. The only one who should be fearful is the devil himself.

"Adjust your thoughts, and you can change your fight."

BE CONSISTENT—BE PERSISTENT

LUKE 18:1-7 (MSG)

I'd better do something and see that she gets justice— otherwise, I'm going to end up beaten black-and-blue by her pounding.

JESUS told them a story showing that it was necessary for them to pray consistently and never give up. He said, "There was once a judge in some city that never gave God a thought and cared nothing for people. A widow in that city kept after him: 'My rights are being violated. Protect me!' He never gave her the time of day. But after this went on and on he said to himself, 'I care nothing what God thinks, even less what people think. But because this widow won't quit badgering me, I'd better do something and see that she gets justice—otherwise I'm going to end up beaten black-and-blue by her pounding.'" [In other words, "Get her off my back!"] "Do you hear what that judge, corrupt as he is, is saying? So, what makes you think God won't step in and work justice for his chosen people, who continue to cry out for help? Won't he stick up for them? I assure you, he will."

The unjust judge was not aware that, though he did not care for God or His people, the widow's consistent and persistent prayers were answered, even if by his irritated response. If an unfair judge responds to the pressures of a nagging widow, how much more would the God who created you be willing to do for you? There are situations in life that require our persistence, not because we do not believe, but because we do. Some issues that we place in the Father's hands by way of prayer keep us in the Master's face to help us continue to maintain our course of action despite what we see. In these times, we can believe that God hears us, and He will answer. Remember this, whatever your prayer request and no matter how long it takes to be answered. Be sure to always let your character be stronger than your circumstance, whether it is an unruly supervisor, a disagreeable spouse, or misbehaved children. Bear in mind that consistency and persistence always attract the One who grants your petitions.

"Prayer promotes allegiance, then protects against a broken spirit."

SAY, "THANK YOU."

LUKE 17:15-16 (NIV)

When one of them saw that he was healed, he came back, praising God in a loud voice. He fell facedown at Jesus' feet in thanksgiving to Him—and he was a Samaritan...

WISE parents always teach their children to have courteous manners. We were taught at least the four basics: *yes, no, please,* and *thank you.* When Chelsea and Jaylon were younger, this was an area of parenting that we did not take lightly, and if for one second we caught them slipping, we addressed it quickly. Good manners go a long way. They are always remembered, like a first impression. Jesus healed all ten lepers, but only one came back to thank Him. We have all witnessed this type of behavior. Maybe you did someone a favor for which you weren't expecting anything in return, but a "thank you" is almost a given. It is possible to receive God's great blessings with an ungrateful heart. God manufactures healing and blessings. It is one of His attributes. I believe He does it without even blinking. God does not demand that we thank Him, nor does He reject us when we do. Our gratefulness is an extension of our personal faith growth. In every growth spurt, we can elevate our knowledge of this great big God which gets us closer to this loving Father who simply wants us, like any good parent, to have proper manners with good behavior. If God never did another thing in our lives, He has surely done more than enough. Remember the cross; it was His only begotten Son.

"Show Him you are grateful by saying, 'Thank you.'"

PLANTED IN STONE

Ezekiel 11:19 (NIV)

I will give them an undivided heart and put a new spirit in them;
I will remove from them their heart of stone
and give them a heart of flesh.

We have all heard the phrase, "Bloom where you are planted," even if that seed has been planted in a hard place. While sitting in the parking lot at church reviewing my lines for the Easter program, music in my ear, I was lost in a worship moment. As I opened my eyes, they zeroed in on this beautiful yellow flower growing between the cracks of the concrete. A seed must produce. I was reminded in this moment that we were once a little tough and rough around the edges. A few of us were even as hard as this concrete where this flower was in full bloom. These facts did not cause God to change His mind about us. In fact, He planted a seed in us before the foundations were formed. These seeds act as a navigational system that will eventually get us to our designated transformation. This radical change is both moral as well as spiritual. Its purpose—to enable us to follow God wholeheartedly. Regardless of your rough path or past, Christ on the third day had the stone rolled away; leaving an empty tomb because He saw ahead to that moment when you recognized you had been redeemed. Your new reality welcomes a new heart, and this heart has new motivations, new desires, and new purposes. Grateful, He looked beyond my faults and saw my needs. Even though there may be days we feel like we are still stuck in the concrete cracks, in due season, we shall see the great harvest He intended.

I read this quote once, "Anyone can count the seeds in an apple, but only God knows how many apples are in a seed." Imagine how many seeds the Father planted in you. Are you ready for your harvest season?

"The stone rolled away, and love found me blooming."

AU FAIT

COLOSSIANS 2:2 (HCSB)

I want their hearts to be encouraged and joined together in love,
so that they may have all the riches of assured understanding
and have the knowledge of God's mystery--Christ.

Short but profound, this French word,
pronounced "oh fe," means *qualified.*

THE QUALIFICATIONS OF JESUS CHRIST
Heals the brokenhearted

Sets the captives free Heals the sick

Restores sight to the blind

Sets at liberty those who are bruised

Founded the earth and established the heavens

Formed man from the dust of the ground

Breathed into man the breath of life

Redeemed man from the curse of the law

Blessings of the Covenant come upon your life through Him

Never been tardy, absent, disobedient, slothful, or disrespectful

Empowers the poor to be poor no more

Can tell you all the secrets of your heart

Has the authority and ability to cleanse you of your sins Laid
down His life so that we may live

Defeated the arch enemy of God and mankind

Miraculously fed the poor and raised the dead

Lends supernatural guidance

Wonderful Counselor—those who listen to Him shall dwell
safely and shall not fear evil

"He is God in the flesh qualified to give us eternal life."

A LITTLE WEEPY

Psalm 126:5 (NIV)

Those who sow with tears will reap with songs of joy.

We met in 1987 when she was 14 and I was 20. I had never met a 14-year-old with such confidence and a goal-oriented mindset. She was doing hair in the basement of their home on Lexington. We had spoken over the phone a few times after I started dating her brother; I loved her immediately. It's safe to say we were instantly sisters. We lived in California, and she lived in Maryland, so we became pen pals, writing letters, sharing our funny life stories, our disappointments. We did not always agree on everything so, yes, we also had a few feuds. I did mention we were sisters, and that's what sisters do sometimes.

Now, let's fast forward to September 23, 2014. My mother-in-law Elvera received her wings in heaven; life just took a drastic change. I was shocked, hurt, in disbelief, and very grieved. When I mustered up the courage to call my sister, upon hearing her voice, my heart hurt so badly. I arrived in Baltimore a few days later, spending as much time as I could with her. The tears as well as the silence are hard to explain. One evening, we sat and talked. I asked her how she was feeling. She responded, "A little weepy." Grief is no laughing matter. It has a state all its own. It is literally a mental suffering or distress from loss–a sharp sorrow. There are very few words to say in times like these, so the best I could offer was just my presence, so I did.

The only one who can heal this void is God Himself. God can restore those empty spaces, and it goes beyond our natural understanding. Grief is not a permanent condition. Sowing is an expression of giving; our tears are seeds that produce a harvest of joy. Only God is able to bring good out of our calamity and loss. God promises the weeping will endure for a night only, then joy comes in the morning. You may cry yourself to sleep every night for a season, but His promise remains: your joy will return, and weepy nights become less frequent. He sees ahead, so I know it is true.

"It's okay to be a little weepy. Grief is not permanent."

UNSEEN ARTILLERY

PSALM 18:2 (KJV)

The LORD is my rock, and my fortress, and my deliverer; my God, my strength, in whom I will trust; my buckler, and the horn of my salvation, and my high tower.

THE armed forces of a country are its government-sponsored defense, fighting organizations for both foreign and domestic policies to defend that body and the nation. In the United States, these forces consist of the Army—they defend on land; the Marines— they attack the land by storming from the sea; the Navy—this bracket of organized defense are stealthy, their moves are strategic, they work undercover; and the Air Force—they handle battles in the air, space, and cyberspace. Lastly, we have the Coast Guard—they defend and protect our coast and the U.S. borders. Their duties are solely to protect, serve, and rescue. God promises to protect those He loves. This is a very big promise, and He loves so many. How does He do it? I propose His militaristic strategy is found in His unseen artillery. Our Commander and Chief is the *rock* that will not be pushed by anyone who wants to harm us. A *fortress* is a safe house which the enemy is unable to get in; we are guarded. The King of Kings is the *buckler (shield)* that stands between us and harmful sabotage, even untimely death. Jehovah Sabaoth is the *horn* of our salvation, His symbol of all power and might. God alone is our *high tower,* formidable above our enemies. When you need protecting, look to God.

"Jehovah Sabaoth uses unseen artillery fearlessly."

NEW THINGS

Isaiah 43:18-19 (ESV)

Remember not the former things, nor consider the things of old. Behold, I am doing a new thing; now it springs forth, do you not perceive it?

Get up...leave...take off... All these words are good ones for those who have been enslaved or, better yet, trapped in the past. In verse 18, Isaiah tells us to forget the former things. If you keep rewinding the tape of the past, you will miss the new good things ahead. God wants us to rely on Him in every area of our lives. God delivered the Israelites from their bondage under the direction of Moses. It is a vivid example of how we should not get comfortable with the things God has already done, because there are more great things that can be done by His command concerning our path. *Exodus* means to retreat or to journey. It sounds to me like we have another choice to make. If we choose to retreat, we are opting for a break. Ask yourself, "How long is my break?" However, if we choose to journey, buckle up for the ride. His ways are higher than ours, so this journey is sure to have moments of big ideas that we just could not have conjured up on our own. For sure, that's when we know it's Him. We must embrace the idea of staying in tune with God, to be led by His spirit, and not to allow our own ideas to get in the way, setting us up for delay. The New Things designed for us are patiently waiting for us to call them forth into our destiny. Life and death are in the power of the tongue *(Proverbs 18:21)*. It is time to start speaking success to your future, declaring those promises that have been spoken over your life to come forth now. My pastor Dr. Fred Hodge says, "If you cannot see it, you cannot have it." Ask the Holy Spirit to help you dream again. Before I write, I always say, "Holy Spirit, I thank you that today I have creative and witty ideas." God is the creator of all things. Since we are made in His image, I have His DNA. I, too, have the gift of creativity. This paper was blank, now it is filled with creative words to inspire you to seek out your *New*.

"Dreaming big, expecting the amazing New Things."

LET IT GLOW

Matthew 5:16 (KJV)

Let your light so shine before men,
that they may see your good works,
and glorify your Father which is in heaven.

Buying your kid's first car is very taxing. Do we purchase new or used? We opted to go with used. After a couple of weeks of shopping, we took a break only to find it in a place we were familiar with. There it was, parked in parking lot of the high school she had just graduated from a year earlier—a silver Toyota Solara. Here is Chelsea's recollection of what took place the day we went to get her car.

Chelsea wrote:

We walked in, and they greeted us as though we were family, complimenting us on our kind manners and great spirit. They mentioned several times that they had many offers on the car, but when they heard my mother's voice, they surely had their minds made up. They loved that she refused to take matters with the car into her own hands, that she wanted to confer with my dad. They stressed that family was a virtue which is why my mom stood out over all the other offers in addition to her bright shining spirit that was practically gleaming over the telephone each time they communicated. My mother used to tell us, "Let your light shine as a child." I remembered asking her after hearing her say it a few times, I decided to ask what did that mean. She explained that in everything we say and do, people should be able to tell that we love God and His Son. I asked her, "So, people should be able to tell we are Christians?" She repeated herself, they should know we love God and His Son not by what we say about our religion, rather how we treat them. I guess my mother's light was shining even over the phone. I will never forget that day, not because I got my first car, but because I witnessed up close my mom live out loud what she had been teaching us every day, and from that day 'til now, I live to let my light shine.

"Illuminate Christ through your life."

MOMMA BEAR ACCESS

PSALM 18:1 (NRSV)

I love you, O LORD, my strength.

HEADED home today after a long day of errands, I stopped at a light only to see an Access van turning in front of me. I heard myself say out loud, "Thankful we are not there anymore." I was speaking of Jay's initial return home. There were wheelchairs, walkers, etc. I was in no way complaining, however, in that moment I could see how far we had come. Yes, it was Jay who had the surgery, but the recovery was an entire family affair. We had to figure out what made the most sense, so we created a routine. I must add that I asked the Holy Spirit to help me figure it out. Five days a week, we battled the 405 freeway in the worst morning traffic. I cannot tell you how many times I cried. Just the driving alone was a nuisance. We applied for Access, a medical driving service. I would drive Jay in the morning, and Access would bring him home in the evening. These were very long days. The point of this short revelation is this, I asked the Holy Spirit to give us a plan, and He did. While it appeared to us that season was long, we all grew up in many areas of our lives. Jay was gaining his independence, and the rest of us learned to really give more of ourselves. We became better listeners, we learned like never before to watch God answer the prayers we had lifted, and we learned how to really pray. As a mother, I learned the term "Momma Bear." Mothers have a love for their children that goes beyond words. Mothers are always in Momma Bear mode, even when there is not a life-changing event happening. Momma bears are loving, cuddly, and protective in a good way, but there is also the ferocious side, when necessary, which makes adjustments when life happens. God is the Poppa bear. His eyes are on all His children at one time.

When life happens, He sees and, like the mother hen, he pulls us closer to Him covering us under His wings as a shelter, a refuge. In closing, a smile came across my face when I thought about the name of the car service, *Access.* This momma bear had complete access to the Poppa who sits on the throne.

"This access gave Momma Bear strength."

PRAYER IS

1 Thessalonians 5:17 (KJV)

Pray without ceasing.

Proposal
Rational—wise/sober
Anointed—appointed/having established your aim
Yield— allow/give way/surrender/obey
Earnest—determined/sincere/expecting
Results—effect/reward/conclusion

PRAYER gives me a legal right, as a daughter of the King, to speak to Him the matters of my heart. In this time, He reveals to me His carefully etched-out plans for my destiny. There is opportunity when we pray. We should not make prayer a begging matter. He is our Father; He already knows what we need. He just wants to be invited to assist us in getting His desire for our lives to come to pass. I understand now why He tells us to come as little children. When our children ask us for things within reason, we quickly respond, "Yes." So, it is with our Father in heaven. He said, "Yes," in Christ from the very beginning, however, there is some work that needs to be done in us and for us. Our children have chores; we do as well. There are levels of maturity that need to take place for our advancement in the spirit. At some point, we must put away the childish things, pick up our cross, and follow His lead. Prayer releases faith and invites God in on His well-planned ideas to lead us to the destiny He desired all along for us to have. There are no filters in Christ, no lukewarm; you're in or out, for Him or against Him. Prayer allows me to stop sitting on my hands and put my heart and hands in His. Prayer releases things I could never obtain without His loving assistance. Prayer is our opportunity to chat with the Father of creation, the One who purposely put us here. Through prayer, His deep mysteries are revealed.

"Speaking to the Master on purpose, for my purpose."

WHY, MOMMA?

1 CORINTHIANS 15:33 (KJV)

Be not deceived: evil communications corrupt good manners.

I REMEMBER when Chelsea was in the 5th grade, I picked her up from school one day. While driving home, she asked an innocent question, "Momma, can I just call you Theresa?" I answered my beautiful daughter swiftly, "No, you may not." The conversation did not end there, of course. She blurted out, "Why not? Well, can I just call you T?" "No!" "But why, Momma? Stacy calls her mom Pat. That's her first name." All the questions were buying me more time to answer. I told her, "You call me Momma because of who I am to you. It is respectful, and you call me Momma because of all I do for you. You call me Momma because it is the right thing to do." Chelsea said, "So, if I called you Theresa, you would stop doing things for me? Would you still love me if I stopped calling you Momma?"

"I am your mother; I will always do things for you, and I will always love you. Nothing can ever change that."

"Momma, I will love you and still be a good daughter even if I called you Theresa."

I began to explain that her calling me by my first name changes the relationship.

"Chelsea, do you remember last year at your birthday party when Stacy drove Ms. Pat's minivan so she could get to your party on time?"

"Yes."

"Would you ever do that?"

"No, Momma."

"That's what I mean about it changing the relationship. Because you obey me as my daughter, calling me by my first name makes me more like your friend than your mother, and you are less likely to respect me in that role. I have also witnessed how she and Ms. Pat talk to one another."

"Oh, I get it."

"I have an idea, let's give each other nicknames. I'll be Blanché. You'll be Madge."

So, it goes with our heavenly Father. If we cannot reverence Him as Lord, it changes the relationship as well as the benefits of being His child. Yes, He will still love us; He said nothing can ever change that.

"Respect in a relationship reaps bountiful benefits."

HIS DNA

1 JOHN 3:1 (NASB)

See how great a love the Father has bestowed on us,
that we would be called children of God; and such we are.
For this reason the world does not know us, because it did not know Him.

WHAT a stunning revelation! This scripture brings to life so many factors. First, if we are His children, and we are, we have our Father's DNA. This reason alone is why Luke tells us that with God, all things have been made possible. If I walk in my full authority by way of His spirit which resides in me, it is impossible for me to fail. Paul emphasizes this fact in Philippians. I can do everything through Him who gives me strength; the power we have received because of our union in Christ is absolute and sufficient to do His will, even when we encounter obstacles that try to distract our view. No, He has not given us superhuman ability to accomplish things in this life, just like we have not given our children any super powers. What we have given them is good, godly directions. Our children have our DNA. They look like us, they speak like us, sometimes they even walk like us. The point is this: He has put the most creative part of Himself inside of us to lead, govern, and guide. We have all heard the saying, "It takes a village," well, there you have it. Our village in the spirit is the Father, the Son, and the Holy Ghost. Children learn by what we teach, but more importantly by what we allow them to see. In the book of John, Jesus says that He can do nothing without the Father. Because of His relationship with the Father, Jesus lived as God wanted Him to live. Our DNA identifies us through Christ. We should start asking ourselves, "What would Jesus do?" He has been an excellent big brother, so we can follow His lead, making intercession for us daily, ensuring that none of us gets lost. He told our Father, "Of those whom You have given Me I lost not one" *(JOHN 18:9)*.

I rest my case. DNA is information used for the transmission of inherited traits.

"His DNA makes all things possible for us."

THE INTRODUCTION

JOHN 14:6 (NIV)

Jesus answered, "I am the way and the truth and the life. No one comes to the Father except through me."

REMEMBER when you were dating someone for the first time? There were exciting moments, filled with butterflies, constant daydreaming, as well as new adventures. After courting a while, they want to introduce you to their family. Your newfound excitement quickly takes an about-face to a nervous belly. You may have thoughts like, "What if they don't like me?" Maybe you even conjured up enough heart to ask your new love interest, "If they don't like me, then what will that mean about us?" Jesus at some point was our newfound love interest, but unlike our natural experience, He quickly wanted us to meet His Father. There was no long period of courting before making this decision. He has been watching us from the beginning, so He knew His Father would approve. If you don't believe in the Son, you never get to meet the Father. Jesus is the way. His sacrifice made Him our salvation. Our salvation granted us the covenant of grace, and He is our possibility to heaven. He is truth itself, in person and character. He is God eternal and really man. Jesus is life; He is the original composer and life-giver. In Him, we live, move, and have our being. We're His offspring. "No one comes to the Father except through me." This introduction has no shortcuts, no secret doors to slip through attempting to approach this sovereign God as an absolute God. Without the mediator's personal touch, such an introduction would not be made possible—no Jesus, no introduction. Jesus, when He first laid eyes on you, fell desperately in love with you, making the decision then that He did not want to just court you. He wanted to spend life with you. He's been waiting patiently for this introduction. When the Father meets us, He knows we love His Son, because Jesus would not have it any other way. He is the *Way,* and He is well-pleased after all His Son has done.

"Your introduction depends on your belief."

BIGGER THAN A WASP

2 Timothy 1:7 (NLT)

For God has not given us a spirit of fear and timidity, but of power, love, and self-discipline.

Anyone who knows me well knows that I am terrified by all manner of insects: tiny, small, large, black, red, yellow, or green. I don't care, I do not want them near me. As a little girl, I would play in the dirt with insects everywhere, and it did not bother me at all. I would catch butterflies, ladybugs, ants. There were times I would even venture off with my brothers to taunt the bees. So, where did this bug phobia begin? My best guess is after seeing a movie in 1998, where this vivacious little boy was obsessed with death. One summer, his fears manifested. He was stung by a swarm of bees and suffered an anaphylactic reaction which resulted in death.

Years later, my parents invited a good friend of mine and me over for dinner at their beautiful, newly-purchased home. The only thing missing was the landscaping. My friend and I decided to go hang out in the landscape-less backyard relaxing, enjoying the sun, and sharing great conversation, when I noticed a wasp, not just one, a few. I quickly scurried to the back door to get in the house for safety. I missed the door by a long shot. I lost my footing, tripped over my feet, and bowled over like I was trying to take first base and score. I literally heard my friend say, "Out!" I landed facedown. My elbows, knees, and hands were bleeding. I looked like I was in a major accident. Once my friend realized I was okay, aside from my external wounds, he blurted, "Out of all that, even if you were stung, your injuries would be less than this."

God has not given us this fear or timidity, so where does it come from? Our mouth speaks, in an open atmosphere, those things that spook us then, over time, we frivolously repeat them. The situation presents itself, and we allow fear to kick in at an all-time high. Fear can be harmful or beneficial. Fear of the Lord is beneficial. It is to reverence this powerful God. The fear that causes harm results in anxiety, worry, even horror. This type of fear disappoints God because it leaves us open to sin. God has given us power. I am bigger than this pest. God's love comes with protection insurance and self-discipline. I have been given enough power to overcome my thoughts about this little phobia. I say little because I am bigger than it.

"Do not allow timidity to cause you to fall."

DON'T GET IT TWISTED

ROMANS 3:23 (NLT)

For everyone has sinned; we all fall short of God's glorious standard.

DON'T get it twisted. Don't believe that some sins are bigger than others simply because they bear obvious severe punishments in the natural world, like a murderer, if caught, goes to prison, whereas a person who lies may just have to deal with a few mad friends. You lust but don't touch, so you're better than the ones who commit adultery. Don't get it twisted, because our sin is lesser we deserve eternal life. All sin makes us sinners, and all sin causes a breach between us and our Holy God. Only Jesus is infallible. Only the Creator is without error. As for the rest of us, we are fallible. We will make mistakes in our flesh, even when we do our best not to. Don't get it twisted by minimizing the small sins and overreacting to the big ones. At the end of the day, both have the same consequence: death. When Paul wrote, *"...we all fall short of God's glorious standard,"* he was expressing that God has rules. One is to be holy, for I Am Holy. There is nothing holy about sin. Standards are an established order. God wants to lavish us in an abundance of blessings, but He can only do this when He sees us; sin covers us up as if we are hiding. Therefore, I will say it once more: don't get it twisted. Be quick to repent, and remember this: you are not alone; everyone has sinned. God knew we would since Adam, so He sent His only begotten Son. So, don't belittle what Christ has done by twisting the facts about sin.

"Sin is sin. All can be forgiven."

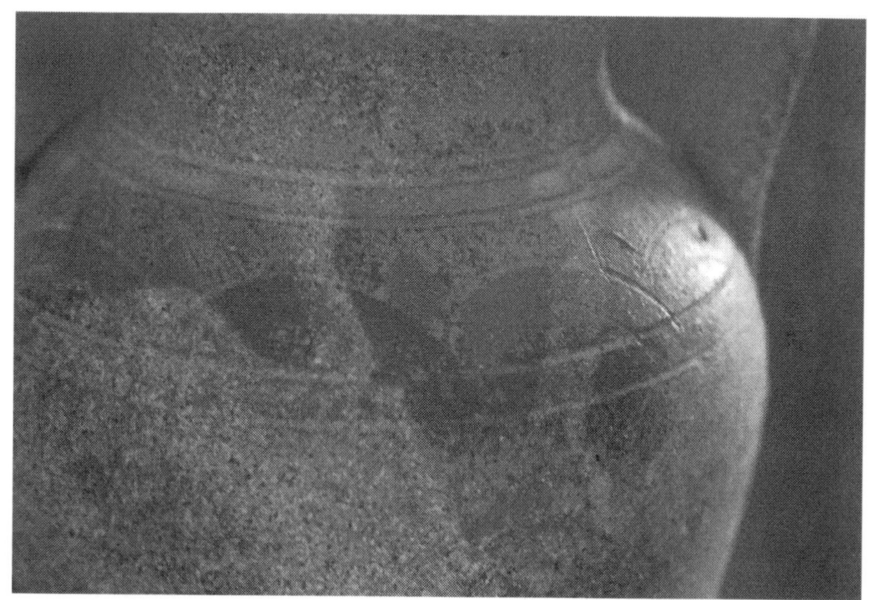

JESUS IS THE MAN

ACTS 17:31 (NIV)

For he has set a day when he will judge the world with justice by the man he has appointed. He has given proof of this to everyone by raising him from the dead.

JESUS, when He rose from the dead, appeared to Mary Magdalene. He quickly told her when she reached out to embrace our Savior, *"Do not hold on to me, for I have not yet ascended to the Father. Go instead to my brothers and tell them, 'I am ascending to my Father and your Father, to my God and your God'"* (JOHN 20:17). He was letting His friend know they both still had work to do. His assignment was to get to His Father so that the Comforter could come. This was urgent to Him. He did not want us to be left here to continue the work of the Kingdom alone. The Holy Spirit is obligated, through Jesus, to help us complete our assignments on the earth. I recently saw a movie where Jesus was lying on a dock with a brokenhearted man. They were gazing up to the star-filled galaxy, when Jesus let out a long sigh and said, "WOW!" as He expressed His amazement at the stars. The man was shocked that the Creator was in awe of His creation. Jesus began to explain to His friend that when He decided to redeem the world, He had to leave heaven in all His glory and have a natural birth to enter this world as a man. In doing this, He would forever see all-natural things just as we do. His divine nature remains; however, He is both deity and human. When He created the galaxies, it was from His divine nature, but as a human being, He sees it from the same perspective as we do. So, yes, He is impressed just like you every time. Jesus is the man in heaven who will judge the world with justice as appointed by the Father, qualified by giving proof of this to everyone who believes He was raised from the dead. Jesus is the only man ever to be resurrected from the grave. Jesus is the only man who was there in the beginning. Jesus is the only man in heaven, and Jesus is the only man whose blood has saving power that never ends.

"Jesus is the man."

POWERFUL, LOVING, & GENTLE

PSALM 23:1 (NIV)

The LORD is my shepherd,
I lack nothing.

POWERFUL ~ ISAIAH 40:10 (NIV)

See, the Sovereign LORD comes with power, and he rules with a mighty arm.
See, his reward is with him, and his recompense accompanies him.

CAREFUL & GENTLE ~ ISAIAH 40:11 (ISV)

Like a shepherd, he tends his flock. He gathers the lambs in his arms,
carries them close to his heart, and gently leads the mother sheep.

GREAT ~ HEBREWS 13:20 (ESV)

Now may the God of peace who brought again from the dead our Lord Jesus,
the great shepherd of the sheep, by the blood of the eternal covenant...

CHIEF SHEPHERD ~ 1 PETER 5:4 (ESV)

And when the chief Shepherd appears,
you will receive the unfading crown of glory.

"Our Shepherd is powerful, loving, gentle, careful, and with Him, we lack nothing."

OUR GOOD SHEPHERD

JOHN 10:11-14 (ESV)

I am the good shepherd. The good shepherd lays down his life for the sheep. He who is a hired hand and not a shepherd, who does not own the sheep, sees the wolf coming and leaves the sheep and flees, and the wolf snatches them and scatters them. He flees because he is a hired hand and cares nothing for the sheep. I am the good shepherd. I know my own and my own know me.

GROWING up, my Dad was always looking for a teaching moment. For the most part, I remember most of those golden nuggets. Here's one I believe is fitting for this scriptural text, "There is a big difference between someone who rents vs. someone who owns. A renter is just passing time and can sometimes be careless with the owner's property since it is not their own, whereas an owner takes extra care of his investment. He has put all that he had into this major purchase."

Jesus our Shepherd is not simply doing a job. He has pledged a lifetime commitment of love and overseeing to the point where He laid down His life for us. His life dictates ownership of ours. On the other hand, you have the hired help who, like the renter, is just passing time for his pay. If another job came along with more pay that would do the trick, he's out, not even giving it a second thought, most likely without even a two-week notice. Jesus' expression is deeply personal. While the hired help runs from danger and the fear of being attacked by the wolf, Jesus has already given His life for all those whom He loves. When He exclaims, *"I know my own and my own know me,"* it reminds me as a mother that in a crowded room with over 100 screaming children, if Chelsea or Jaylon were somewhere in that same room, I would hear their cry, their laugh, or their screams; after all, they are mine.

"Our Good Shepherd is a lifetime owner."

BITTER TO THE ROOT

Hebrews 12:15 (ESV)

See to it that no one fails to obtain the grace of God; that no "root of bitterness" springs up and causes trouble, and by it many become defiled

BITTERNESS springs up first in our minds, this is where the seed is planted, and then it germinates in our hearts. The problem here is that, like any seed that grows, it gets roots. Bitterness grows its roots, and it manifests unforgiveness and begins to breed a grudge. This bitter grudge causes a separation—a separation between you and the only One that is able to give you the grace needed to set you free.

The sequoia tree is the largest living tree in the world. Its roots start small, however, over time, they grow to support its structure. The roots expand for miles, sometimes compromising the other living trees in the forest. God always speaks on purpose. Using the word defiled is no accident, and bitterness has the ability to contaminate others in our lives. Bitterness sets us up for failure that we are so unaware of, because in the onset of this massive ugly root, we initially feel justified by the hurt we experienced, thinking we need to handle it on our own. You know the saying, "Just what the doctor ordered?" I will say it this way, "Just what the devil planned." We are created by a creative God made in His image. Our creative minds erect the perfect tapestry of the insult. We agree that it is our best work, therefore, we hold on to it. When we hold on to things we do not have the capacity to handle, we are in danger yet again. We are not holding on to God's unchanging hand, not allowing His sufficient grace to complete its redemptive and complete work. We are made in His image. Can you imagine what a bitter god would look like? I can't, nor do I want to. I will keep the forgiving, always-loving, full-of-mercy God. He loves us and wants us free. I do not mean to use clichés, however, in this case it is suited perfectly, "Let go, and let God."

"Let the Creator start at the roots."

WHEN I SIT TO WRITE

LAMENTATIONS 3:27-28 (HCSB)

It is good for a man to bear the yoke while he is still young. Let him sit alone and be silent, for God has disciplined him.

To *"bear the yoke while he is still young"* is to come under God's discipline and let Him teach us, for we all know as we get older, we are more likely to be set in our ways and do things out of custom. We cannot stop trials from coming. We live in a world that is full of them. There are wars in the world we have no control over, there are feuds among us, poverty, perversion, death, sorrow, and a nation where 13-million children do not get enough to eat. Though it appears there is nothing we can do, as believers, we have the Father's listening ear.

When I sit to write, I write to sit. This sitting process involves many crucial components. First, I must get silent. When the Teacher is speaking, I get my best results by listening. Second, I have a heart of repentance. Light and darkness cannot dwell together, and I need Him to speak. Lastly, I have to put patience on the table and have complete confidence that wisdom will begin to teach me the mysteries and knowledge that outside of Him I would not obtain. When I sit to write, I write to sit. I dare to just jot down my own thoughts without His assistance. I am writing for the purposes of lives changing, and who would be a better teacher than the One who authored the Book? In this same manner, because He answers when we pray. We have eyes to see all the calamity in this corroding world. To sit back and do nothing is disheartening to such a loving God. Sure, He's God, however, He gave man dominion over the earth, so we must invite Him into this mess. Can you imagine if every believer looked outside of their circumstances and began to pray for the sick, vile things we witness every day? It wouldn't be heaven, but I believe we would be close. Start sitting.

"Take a lesson from Mary: start sitting at His feet."

PESKY VERMIN

Proverbs 2:6 (ESV)

For the LORD gives wisdom;
from his mouth come knowledge and understanding

Last summer, a church in my neighborhood began doing upgrades to their building. This building sat in the middle of quite a bit of property. Well, let me begin with this: the excavating disturbed a lot of little creepy critters. I am certain of this, because these now-homeless critters began looking for a new place. Watching television one evening just before the sun was completely down, I saw something scamper across my back fence, but since we have lots of lizards, I quickly dismissed it. A few hours later, I didn't see it, but I darn sure heard it, and it did not sound like a lizard. I thought it could be a cat. I flipped on the backyard lamps, and it was as if the critter was saying to me, "I dare you to come back here." It did not budge. Instead, it just stared as I stared back. I thought, "Someone is not going to sleep tonight, and that someone would be me."

In the morning, I made a beeline to the hardware store for mouse traps. Jay put the traps out. In anticipation, I just sat quietly, waiting to hear them start snapping. Hours later, still nothing. It wasn't until I was comfortable, thinking maybe they found another yard, only to be startled when I heard the snap but also a struggle. Looking out of my patio door, I screamed for Jay. This was no little mouse, this was a *RODENT* on another scale. Jay and I rushed back to the hardware store to get more traps but this time larger ones.

This went on for weeks. Finally, one evening, I asked the Lord to please help me get rid of these pesky vermin. I heard in my spirit two things. First, I was waiting for you to ask, and second, you're using the wrong traps. Once you ask for wisdom, He will walk you through the entire process, and that He did. I followed the instructions, and within two days, the pesky vermin were in the bottom of the garbage can outside, waiting for the garbage truck to take them away on the next pickup day. The Lord gave the wisdom, and I obtained new knowledge. You must know your target so you use the right bait. In this case, the bait that got the job done was called Catchmaster® Snap Traps. The traps I had purchased before this new information were Tomcat® traps, but tomcats like to play around. When you have a serious situation, you need the wisdom and knowledge of the Catchmaster. The problem could have been solved sooner had I asked for wisdom and knowledge in the first place.

"Don't torture yourself. Seek wisdom to get rid of what's pestering you."

RECOVERY

1 PETER 5:10 (ESV)

And after you have suffered a little while, the God of all grace,
who has called you to his eternal glory in Christ,
will himself restore, confirm, strengthen, and establish you.

WHEN Jay had his consultation for brain surgery, he asked his surgeon how long before he would be himself again. My heart sank, but I kept a straight face and gazed over at his dad, whose heart was sinking just like mine, remembering that God Himself would restore Jay and give him the strength to get through this season. Dr. Mortazavi told Jay they like to have their patients up the next day, getting them to walk and do a few other rehabilitating exercises to see if the brain recalls what it used to do on a normal basis. The day after Jay's surgery, he did get up, though he hardly spoke. I kept reminding myself that this was part of the recovery process. I recalled a conversation with Jay's neuro-nurse where I asked her why it was taking so long for us to see any big changes. She explained Jaylon's body had lived with this malformation for 19 years. Up to now, that had been his whole life. The foreign object that had been removed was missing from his body, and now his body was trying to figure out how to live without it. It was trying to recover from this missing, though foreign, malformation. I would like to ask you a few questions: What have you recently let go of that's been with you a long time? Where are you in your recovery? Are you fully restored?

Restoration/Recovery: the restoration or return to any former and better state or unimpaired condition. Everything we experience in life will be used for the glory of God, even Jay's malformation. In this case, God was not only healing Jay's body, He also promised to strengthen us. He gave each of us the adequate amount to willingly do our part, then He established us, meaning He made sure that when this recovery process ended, we would each have a testimony to share of His goodness. Though we all had a few, "Are you serious God?" moments, restoration was never off the table. He is the King of recovery.

"Who has called you to his eternal glory in Christ, will himself restore."

SPEAK TO THEM MOUNTAINS

Matthew 17:20 (ESV)

He said to them, "Because of your little faith. For truly, I say to you, if you have faith like a grain of mustard seed, you will say to this mountain, 'Move from here to there,' and it will move, and nothing will be impossible for you."

The Alps Mountains were formed over tens of millions of years as the African and Eurasian *tectonic plates* collided. Extreme shortening caused by the event resulted in marine *sedimentary rocks* rising by *thrusting* and *folding* into high mountain peaks such as *Mont Blanc* and the *Matterhorn.* Mont Blanc spans the French-Italian border, and at 15,781 feet, is the highest mountain in the Alps. The Alpine region contains about one-hundred peaks higher than just over 13,000 feet.

Notice, the title does not say *Mountain,* it says *Mountains.* I believe that many of us have more than one mountain standing in our way. The disciples were agitated that they were unable to cast the demon out, so they pulled Jesus to the side to ask, "Why couldn't we do that?" Jesus said, "It's your lack of faith." We must remember that it is the power of God, not our Faith, that moves mountains, however, faith must be somewhere in the vicinity for them mountains to budge. Mustard seed is the smallest particle conceivable. I think Jesus was low-key saying tiny faith or underdeveloped faith would be better than what you boys got, and it would have worked. Obviously, Jesus is telling us this power is so potent a little bit goes a long way. There is great power in even a little faith provided we take God with us. Remember, we are free agents; we have to ask for His help. Maybe the disciples, for a split second, allowed arrogance to creep in. We can learn a lesson from these boys. Our ability to do great exploits like moving mountains cannot be done by our own natural ability. I mentioned that many of us have a few mountains we need to command to move from here to there. Just as the Alps each have names and different sizes like the Matterhorn and Mont Blanc, name them all. Be specific. Maybe your mountain is insecurity or abandonment. It could be finances. Whatever it is, call it out, but before you do, I encourage you to exercise your faith. Invite the Holy Spirit to join you with all power then say, "Mountains, move from here to there. Dunamis, or miraculous power, raised Jesus from the dead.

"He has given us dunamis power to move our mountains."

I'M HUNGRY

CORINTHIANS 12:25 (ESV)

...that there may be no division in the body,
but that the members may have the same care for one another.

I KNOW that this scripture is referring to the operation of the Church, however, just go with me as I use it to illustrate the function of our natural bodies. If my feet hurt, they will cause my stride to be a bit slower than usual. A headache, upset stomach, whatever ails my body throws the rest of my members off. That is why there is medicine and prayer. It is not God's will for us to suffer, even if it is for a little while, so our bodies must function the way the Father designed them to. The way God designed our bodies goes beyond amazing.

A week after Jay's brain surgery, he was still not up and about, however, he was fully aware of his surroundings, who we were, and he did his best to communicate. Jay was so aware that he recalled his surgeon telling him in consultation that the day after surgery, the plan was to have him up and walking. Jay was aggressively trying to get out of the bed and walk. The brain is amazing at recalling. Being the inquisitive person that I am, I started drilling the nurses. There were so many tubes and IV bags, I was certain that one must have been feeding my son. I asked his nurse how many nutrients Jay was getting. Her reply stunned me, "None." "What do you mean? It has been 10 days. Are you really telling me my son has not eaten in 10 days?" I felt sick, and she knew it. My eyes were full of tears ready to fall. Stephanie, that was her name, began to explain to me that he was not hungry. I asked her how she could be sure. She said that part of his brain was not awake yet. I was a bit baffled. She said with the brain surgery, many members of the body have been affected like his speech, his ability to walk, and the use of his hands. There are chambers in the brain for each function of the body and because of the surgery, the brain felt compromised. It was in a state of trauma. As it begins to realize that what has taken place was for his good, it will start to wake up and properly function the correct way, beginning the healing process. "How will we know when that happens?" I said. She replied, "Jay will let us know." While I was relieved to know my son was not starving, I anticipated the day he would let us know.

Four days later, Jay reached for my hand and whispered, "I'm hungry." So, it goes with our walk with Christ. When we all function the way God purposed, every member benefits to His full glory.

"Who has called you to his eternal glory in Christ, will himself restore."

GOING LIVE

PSALMS 27:1 (ESV)

The LORD is my light and my salvation; whom shall I fear?
The LORD is the stronghold of my life; of whom shall I be afraid?

THE age of technology has come a long way, from email to webcams, and in 2002, social media began to emerge. Initial social sites like Friendster and MySpace were just places you could go to chat with friends, meet new friends, and post pictures. Facebook began in 2003, and in 2006, Twitter evolved where you could post short thoughts about whatever you wanted to share. In 2010, FaceTime came around, and you could talk face-to-face over the phone. Well, I was good with all of the above.

In 2016, the world was introduced to Periscope and Facebook Live, where you could have your own live audience letting them in on your world, sharing what you wish. I am a teacher. I'm often asked to facilitate events or be mistress of ceremonies. I am also a minister, so speaking in front of an audience should be no big deal, but it was. What the heck was I afraid of? I mean, I get a nauseating kind of fear, cold sweats, clammy palms, and ultimately a dry throat. I sound like a man, so I just shut up. When asked why I had never gone "live," I would always reply, "It kind of freaks me out. Speaking into the camera and not seeing faces is not for me. What if I don't gain an audience, and what if they don't like what I have to say?"

Then one day, I got a call from the church office, and Brandi was on the other end. "Min T., pastors want to know if you could host a webinar tonight on health?" Without hesitation I accepted, and I did it. When, weeks later, they asked again, I had two live webinars under my belt. When I finished that night, Willa, my publisher and friend, who's been pushing me to jump over this minor hurdle to go "live" for quite a while now, called. "You did great. Can I ask a question: what's the difference?" I never let her finish her question. I knew where she was going, but most importantly, what I needed to do. God is my salvation, my stronghold, the One who called me to do what I do. He had my pastors ask me to host so I would overcome this minor hurdle and allow these devotions to be written and verbally heard.

P.S. I had close to 300 viewers, even a few book sales!

"2017, I overcame my fears. This author went 'live.'"

I JUST ATE

Proverbs 19:17 (ESV)

Whoever is generous to the poor lends to the Lord, and he will repay him for his deed.

I STARTED over two years ago on what I call healthy habits—a lifestyle change for me to take better care of my temple. Chelsea and Jaylon are pretty healthy and athletic; I wanted to keep up with them but also, to be around for them, so I made a drastic change. Many began to compliment me on the results. One friend said, "Minister T., you should take before and after pictures and post them. You could really help a lot of people." I will admit it took me a few days, but I finally followed through. To my surprise, I hadn't even noticed what I had accomplished until I saw the pictures.

Fast forward—as a result of the pictures I had posted to my social media, a few people reached out and asked if I would be willing to help them make this lifestyle change. I conceded. A few months in, Felicia and I had been working out 3-4 days a week together swimming, hiking, kickboxing, speed walking, you name it, we tried it. One summer morning, she called to suggest instead of kickboxing, we exercise at the beach. I told her that was fine, we would meet halfway. My only concern was I had my lunch made already. Part of my healthy regimen is that I make my own food. I told her, "No worries. I will bless someone today with my lunch." "Who?" she asked. "I don't know, but that's the plan."

Leaving the beach, I saw who I was giving my lunch to. There was a homeless gentleman with a sign. Eager to give him this nicely-chilled lunch, we approached him. He had a smile in his eyes when he saw us coming, however, when I told him I wanted to give him my good lunch, he looked like he wanted to kick rocks. Instead, he mumbled under his breath, "I just ate," and refused my generous offer. Felicia laughed so hard, we had to pull over. I, on the other hand, was not laughing, at least not at first, but as Felicia kept repeating it with that same mumble, the laughter became infectious. I guess I will have to go with what Pastor Hodge told me a few years ago, "Do what God tells you. Don't be concerned how they accept it, because heaven records your actions." If you help the poor, you are lending to the LORD—and he will repay you!

"Felicia writes from time to time #homelessguydidntwantMintlunch."

THIS IS HOW YOU DO IT

MATTHEW 6:9-13 (NIV)

This, then, is how you should pray: "Our Father in heaven, hallowed be your name, your kingdom come, your will be done, on earth as it is in heaven. Give us today our daily bread. And forgive us our debts, as we also have forgiven our debtors. And lead us not into temptation, but deliver us from the evil one."

HERE is another perfect illustration of how much God just adores His children. Remember when you were a child, your grandmother or mother taught you how to pray? I do. In this moment with His disciples, Jesus is doing the same. He is teaching them how to pray, the most effective way to get the results God desires them to have. It is entitled "The Lord's Prayer" because it was Jesus who taught it as He was preparing them for when He would not physically be with them. Today, many people just say this prayer out of tradition, as if it were something to just recite because somewhere along the way, someone made them learn it. There is so much more to this prayer than just rehearsed lines.

Our Father—We acknowledge Him as Lord.

in heaven,—He dwells in the heavens, but He is close enough to hear us because He loves us.

hallowed be your name,—We are honoring His great names; His name alone has vindicated our lives.

your kingdom come, your will be done on earth as it is in heaven.—We accomplish His desired plans on earth as He orchestrates them from heaven for our abundance on earth.

Give us today our daily bread.—Daily, we see brand new mercies, and all our needs are supplied.

And forgive us our debts (sins), **as we also have forgiven our debtors** (others).—If we forgive, we are forgiven by the Father.

And lead us not into temptation, but deliver us from the evil one.—We are not consumed by the enemy's plots. We all will have times of temptation, but we do not have to give in. When we understand it is part of the enemy's plot, God through Jesus has already paid so much for us. He does not want any of His children to run off with His enemy.

"The Lord's prayer, intentionally powerful."

PRAYER MADE THE DIFFERENCE

COLOSSIANS 4:2 (NLT)

Devote yourselves to prayer with an alert mind and a thankful heart.

SEVERAL years ago, in a leadership at my former church of 12 years, Pastor Bob asked us, "Do you pray every day over your families?" He went further and asked, "Do you pray together as a family?" A few said, "Yes," but my answer was, "No." He said, "Sister Theresa, it is very important you don't leave the house without covering each member of your family." The way he said it, I will be honest, it kind of scared me, especially since I was the only one who thought this was like a *wow* moment. The very next day, before leaving for work, I prayed, just like Pastor Bob instructed. I prayed for my children, who were only in daycare at the time. That should let you know how long ago I came to understand that prayer makes the difference. Chelsea is 24, and Jaylon is 22, now. On my drive home from work that day, I saw Pastor Bob in the back of a police car while I was stopped at a light on Pearblossom Highway. I waved to catch his attention, to make sure he was okay. He assured me he was fine. He was doing a drive-along with the local sheriff 's department. On Sunday, when we arrived at church, Pastor Bob had one of the deacons come and get me stating that Pastor wanted to see me. When I went into his office, he began to tell me about his history with the sheriff's department, but most importantly, he wanted me to hear this: "Sister Theresa, the other day when we saw each other on the highway, right after you turned left onto Sierra Highway, the next vehicle that was stopped at that very place you were was hit head-on. The driver did not survive." I was speechless. In that very moment, I experienced the same feeling I had in the meeting where he instructed us to pray over each other. I told my Pastor that was the first day I prayed over my family before leaving home, just as he had instructed. He said, "Sister Theresa, prayer made the difference."

"Prayer covers the unseen things."

BAD REP

CORINTHIANS 5:20 (ESV)

Therefore, we are ambassadors for Christ,
God making his appeal through us.
We implore you on behalf of Christ, be reconciled to God.

WE have all been there; the day is just too much, and overwhelmed is an understatement. I had a doctor's appointment, and I was not happy with the information I received today. "Mrs. Kirk, your lab results are positive for cancer in your uterus. Further testing will be required to determine your course of treatment." My mind was racing. I could not concentrate, and the possibility of cancer freaked me out.

Trying to get it together, I went to the market to grab a few things for dinner; I decided on fish. I got to the butcher counter and asked the clerk for the fish I wanted. He appeared to be having a bad day. His service stank, and I was not in the mood for it. I snapped. I made sure he knew today was not the day to get on my nerves. Then, to top it off, I positioned myself to try to get the approval of other patrons to agree with my nasty attitude. I embarrassed the clerk, myself, but most importantly, Christ.

My heart sank. I felt awful, but my pride allowed me to rationalize my behavior. I clearly heard the Holy Spirit tell me to go apologize. My stubbornness said otherwise. I got home that evening, still vexed in my spirit for my behavior. It bothered me for over a week. The Holy Spirit will not allow you to get away with absurd shenanigans. "He literally said you are a bad rep." I could no longer reason over this foolishness; God just told me I was a bad rep.

While driving to the store, I found myself still saying things like, "Okay, God, if that's you, then the clerk will be there when I arrive," as if the devil would ever tell you to apologize or that you are a bad rep. I got to the store and made my way to the meat counter. I saw him, and he saw me. I knew this because his face turned beet red. I approached the counter and asked him if I could speak with him. He reluctantly conceded. I told him that I apologized for my behavior, that I was a Christian, and my behavior that day was poor and inexcusable. I further explained by telling him about that day-where I was mentally-but that was still no excuse for the way I treated him. His name is Mason. When I go to the market now, he speaks as though we are friends. One day, he approached me saying, "Theresa, your apology that day changed my life."

Revelation: follow the instructions of the Holy Spirit.

"Ambassadors must be led by the Holy Ghost. He's in the life changing business."

BE A WITNESS

John 1:8 (NIV)

He himself was not the light;
he came only as a witness to the light.

I AM definitely a fan of word games like crossword puzzles and Scrabble®. My favorite is Word Chums®. Margo, my opponent, lives in London, England. Randomly one day, she used the chat feature simply to say, "Hello." The day she decided to chat, I was sitting with Chelsea at the hospital, the two of us exhausted as we watched Jay sleep in his hospital room. A few days later she wrote again to tell me that she would not be able to play for a few days because her husband was ill. They had to travel for him to get a diagnosis and a treatment plan, and she was requesting my prayers. How did she know I was a believer? I quickly responded by sending her a prayer that would cover them both.

A week or so later, she sent another chat, this time asking if I needed prayers for anything. I explained Jay's recent surgery. She went on, saying her husband John's diagnosis was colon cancer and, because he was an elderly man, their treatment for him was limited. She asked for me to just pray that he would not suffer long and for her family's peace during this time. Margo told me she and John had been married over 50 years and that she would be devastated if he did not survive. I encouraged her as much as I could through the word and prayer. I heard her heart through the words she had endearingly written.

The word *witness* indicates our role as reflectors of Christ's light. Jesus is the true light. He helps us to see our way and, in return, we are to direct others using the same light He has allowed us to carry. I believe this was the transaction—it was the light that illuminated for Margo, the prayers reflected the light of Christ. A few months had gone by, and I had not heard from Margo, so I prayed all was well. After a few days, I had a new game request. I accepted. It was Margo's daughter explaining to me her father passed away a week earlier on his birthday. However, her mother wanted to thank me for my prayers, that she was positive they worked, and she wanted to get an update on Jay. Periodically, I get a message from Margo, which always warms my heart just to know that she's doing well, but mostly that I am a witness to the prayers that God answered concerning her broken heart.

"The light of Christ has healing reflectors."

KIND HUMAN BEING

1 CORINTHIANS 13:4 (NIV)

Love is patient, love is kind.
It does not envy, it does not boast, it is not proud.

ATLANTA bound, but for now, I'm on a layover in Houston, Texas. I scurry to the ladies' room. While at the vanity as we wash our hands, I notice her gazing in my direction. I don't pay much attention to it initially, until she whispers, "You are a patient woman. I don't know how you did it." I quickly realize she must have been on the flight where I met Lou. I respond, "I did not mind. He was very sweet, and I enjoyed our chat. He recently lost his wife and just wanted to talk." She is stuck for a moment as she dries her hands, and then as she passes to leave, she gently puts her hand on my shoulder. Not whispering this time around, she says, "You are not only patient, but you are a kind human being. Wow."

I walk out of the ladies' room smiling, not out of pride, but because I am thinking, "I bet that made God smile. Is that why they put me on that particular flight?" You see, my original flight was at 7:50 a.m. There was an accident on the freeway, and there was nothing the commuter bus could do. We all had to ride this one out. But God always has a bigger idea than we could ever imagine. I always welcome these sweet surprises. She was calling me patient because Lou was hard of hearing, so on that two hour fifty-one-minute flight, each time I spoke or the pilot said something over the intercom, his response was the same in his 86-year-old voice, *"WHAT?"*

While boarding the bus, they ask you what airline. When I stated this to the luggage guy and then the driver, they both had this ominous look on their faces. Then I heard a passenger say, "That's the last terminal." I was doing my best not to panic. It was 6:00 a.m. Clearly, we would get there in time. Well, just like God placed me right next to Lou, he placed me on this bus next to a feisty woman from Brooklyn, New York, who travels often. She offered me a few of her wise travel tips for LAX. "Sweetie, what time's your flight?" I told her. "Here's what you do. At the first terminal, get off, cross over the airport parking structures, but do me a favor, just don't get hit." Well, I made it to the airport terminal with only 15 minutes 'til that aircraft was taking off. So, the nice lady at the airline concierge obliged me by putting me on another flight that would still get me to my destination at its intended and original time. I did not have to make any adjustments or make any calls to disrupt anyone's day because I panicked. Instead, I counted on the prayers I prayed in the morning. After all, He answers when we pray, so I'm covered on this flight and the ones to come. Fancy that. I'm a kind human being.

"Who's watching or listening to you?"

GOD IS LISTENING BUT NOT ANSWERING

1 Samuel 28:6-7 (NKJV)

And when Saul inquired of the LORD, the LORD did not answer him, either by dreams or by Urim or by the prophets. Then Saul said to his servants, "Find me a woman who is a medium, that I may go to her and inquire of her." And his servants said to him, "In fact, there is a woman who is a medium at Endor"

We have seen the commercials and the billboards. We have even had friends who dabbled a little, when impatient, because they were anxious to know what their future held. It feels like this is the quickest way to get a glance at our road ahead. There are a few things I personally just refuse to play around with, such as psychic hotlines, tarot cards, or mediums, but that's just me.

Saul messed up big time. Samuel was instructed by God to anoint Saul king and to have Saul destroy all that God commanded him to destroy. Saul was disobedient. This grieved God greatly; therefore, God stopped all communication with Saul. When fear entered Saul's heart, he needed direction, but God was not talking. Saul had banned all mediums and psychics from the land, but in desperation, he turned to one for counsel. Under his command, he ordered this practice removed from the land; however, he did not remove it from his heart. The witch of Endor hesitant initially, conceded and honored Saul's request, channeling Samuel for direction since God was silent. Samuel was quite irritatedbut told Saul by way of the witch he and his sons would be with him the next day. If God told the Israelites not to fool around with sorcery, mediums, witchcraft, and divination, He is also saying the same to us. When we seek direction from sources outside of God, it grieves God. He will never reveal His will or plans to these outside sources. He speaks to us through His own channels: His Word, His Son, and His Holy Spirit.

"Quit speaking to dead things, when you have a living King."

HE IS OVER IT

ISAIAH 43:25 (NLT)

I-yes, I alone-will blot out your sins for my own sake and will never think of them again.

WHY torture yourself with your past mistakes? If the creator Himself makes it clear that He is over it, we should give ourselves a break and do the same. Understanding that God knows all and sees all, He chooses to limit Himself in this area of our lives. What a gracious and loving God!

In the book of *MICAH,* He tells us that He throws them into the sea of forgetfulness. Imagine for a moment how many things have been lost at sea never to be found. In *HEBREWS,* He uses the writers to tell us He forgives our wickedness and will remember our sins no more. Sounds to me like He is yet again expressing He is over it. In *PSALMS,* He declared as far as the east is from the west, He has removed our transgressions from us, therefore stating that we are the ones who allow our minds to repeat our past offenses.

He states that He does this for His own sake. In other words, if He did not limit Himself in this area, He would have to carry out a wrath on us for our sinful ways. When He says He never thinks of them again, He is making a strong choice to not ponder on our mistakes. Sin separates us from this loving God. He does not want or like to be separated from His children. What parent does? We are humans born with sin in our very nature. That is why the redemptive work on the cross through Jesus is truly God's greatest creative work; it is in this that the brand-new mercies we get daily have been made possible.

Let me be clear: the amazing forgiveness we receive only works when we are quick to ask for it, while at the same time staying in a forgiving state as well. Our Adamic nature likes to hold on to offenses. We even remind our offender of their past mistakes, but when God forgives our sins, He totally forgets them. We need never be concerned about God reminding us of them later. When Jesus was on the cross, He asked the Father to forgive His offenders. Take a lesson from the cross forgive quickly, and when your mind starts to repeat your past, declare out loud, "He's already over it, therefore, today, I am too."

"Get over it. God already has."

MEDITATION BREEDS

PSALM 1:2 (ESV)

But they delight in the law of the LORD,
meditating on it day and night.

WHEN you assemble things, you must follow the instructions. In my first devotional, I talked about the "cake mix theory." In it I express the importance of following the directions and using the right ingredients. One wrong step could cause your baked goods not to rise. So, it goes with meditating. What we focus on intentionally, we bring to full manifestation good or bad, happy or sad; we have the utmost authority to bring these things to pass.

Meditation defined is to engage in thought or contemplation; to reflect. The psalmist writes, "*...but his delight is in the law of the LORD, and on his law he meditates day and night.*" In other words, the reader takes pleasure and respects His decrees for our living and, more importantly, has a desire to please Him with their life. There is no better way to accomplish this than to follow His guide to assembling our lives. Knowing His word and meditating on it are key steps to applying it daily in our lives. To follow God completely, we must know what He says. The more you know, the better you will be able to obey, making the best decisions to live your best in Him. In the full scope of things, when we delight in His presence, we are certain to be more fruitful. *Breed* means to produce. When we engage or reflect on God's word, it produces His expected end, and we know that all His plans are good for us. Let us begin meditating so we can start truly producing.

"Meditation creates manifestation."

STAY CLOSE

PROVERBS 8:35 (NIV)

For those who find me find life
and receive favor from the LORD.

STARTING over is not always easy, even for the strongest person. I always use the phrase, "I am a creature of habit," so you can imagine, I don't like sudden changes. I believe God was telling me, "That is not any way to live. Change is good. Change opens new doors of opportunity. Change exposes you to you." After 30 years, I am filing my taxes as a single person. Trying to decide where I should go, I asked friends for referrals. I got a few when I decided not to make this task a major deal and just go to local CPA in my area I made appointments at two different places on the same day for different times. The day of the appointments, I could not make up my mind, so I asked the Holy Spirit to tell me what to do. I clearly heard Him say, "Stay close."

Let me explain. The local CPA was around the corner. The other place was an hour away, so I canceled that one and did as He said. I stayed close. The other difference between these two places, besides the distance, was their price points. The L.A. referral had a set price that I could easily manage, but the one around the corner could not tell me until they completed the work. This was unsettling, but I know I heard, "Stay close." I arrived at my appointment on time, however the CPA I was scheduled to see was running behind, so they assigned someone else to work on my books. I asked again for a price, still nothing. Alia the CPA was very friendly, helpful, and even polite. Suddenly, just when she was completing my taxes, their computers froze, so we were left to chat. The computers were back up and running. Apologizing for my long wait, Alia blurted out, "That will be $348.00." I responded without blinking, "I should have driven to L.A." For a minute, Alia did not say a word. Then she took my papers and typed vigorously for about 10 minutes. She handed over my taxes and said, "Thank you for your business. It was a pleasure to meet you." I said, "What do I owe you?" She said, "Nothing." Change was a good idea that day. My original CPA was changed. I changed my perspective about distance and pricing. I trusted God with that. He said, "Stay close," and I did.

"Favor and taxes can be in the same sentence, just stay close."

NO REGRETS

SAMUEL 15:11 (ESV)

"I regret that I have made Saul king, for he has turned back from following me and has not performed my commandments." And Samuel was angry, and hecried to the LORD all night.

I RECENTLY posted on my Facebook page, "When God tells you to do something, do not try to alter it." When God gives instructions, trust and believe He has a greater purpose than you can begin to imagine.

Saul's saga is the perfect example. Let's be clear, God's regret was not because He made a mistake. God is omniscient. He is unable to make mistakes. The word *regret* here is to reflect His sorrow over His decision to make Saul king, because Saul instantly got a big head and wasted no time doing it. Samuel became angry. His anger resulted in a restless night once the Lord expressed how He felt, so he got up early the next morning to go give gangster Saul a piece of his mind. Saul was ghost—he had gone over to another town called Carmel to have a monument set up in his own honor. When God gives us a plan, it is not about us. It is always about Him, and we should never turn the tables and seek to be honored. His purposes are to always point back to Him. Saul had turned God's interests into his own. He allowed his heart to change towards God, and it grieved God. Ultimately, his disobedience caused a major breach between him and the Lord. When we disobey the plans of God, we open the door for so many other self-destructive behaviors to set in, taking us further away from the Father's heart and His plans. Every great and creative idea that is much bigger than you has to be a God idea. Just go with it so you can live a life without regret while at the same time making the heart of God happy. He chose you without regret.

"No regrets when I go with His plans."

ROCK CLIMBING REVELATIONS

PROVERBS 3:5-6 (KJV)

Trust in the LORD with all thine heart;
and lean not unto thine own understanding.
In all thy ways acknowledge him, and he shall direct thy paths.

My birthday was fast approaching. Planning my big day, I had all kinds of ideas for new adventures I wanted to experience. I was watching some show on TV when on the show the characters were rock climbing. "Hmm," I thought, "I'd like to try that." I asked Jay if he would like to go. He said he did not think he was ready for that, so I started thinking of other things he, Chelsea, and myself could do that none of us had done before, but rock climbing is where I had my mind made up.

A few days later, I received a text from a close friend asking what was I going to do for my birthday. When I replied saying, "I don't know yet," Liza replied, "Have you ever rock climbed?" I was over the moon with excitement. I was going to do it, exactly what I wanted to do. I invited a few other girlfriends; it was now a concrete date. Once we arrived, I realized I had no idea what I had just set myself up for but I was going to stick it out. With harnesses secure, chalk-covered hands, weird rock climbing shoes, and one demonstration by a pro, we were set to scale a few walls. Brandi, Kalies, Nikki, and Liza had successfully made it to the top. I was stuck in the middle looking down, afraid to go down. Everyone was supporting me down below, but I was screaming, "I can't!"

I finally blundered my way to the ground, but I was shaken for second. By the way, I never made it to the top of that wall. Liza and Nikki came up with this grand idea that I should try climbing another wall, one that did not require a harness. I thought they had lost their minds, but I decided to follow their lead and go for it. Shaking and nervous, I made it to the top without a harness. On this wall, you don't come down, you scale over. Once at the top, my emotions got the best of me, and I began to cry. I just had a rock climbing revelation: as long as I had the safety of the harness, I put my trust in it, however, going up and trusting God to get me there, I put my life in His hands allowing Him to direct my path. Rock climbing walls have paths and patterns to follow to help you get to the top. Letting the harness go allowed me not to lean on my own knowledge or to put my trust in it. What harnesses are you putting your trust in?

"Acknowledge Him on your way to the TOP."

CABIN FEVER

Proverbs 3:5-6 (ESV)

Trust in the LORD with all your heart,
and do not lean on your own understanding.
In all your ways acknowledge him, and he will make straight your paths.

Heading south for a few days, I must admit I'm excited to see what's in store for me on this week's journey. I have great expectations, that's for sure. The first two days will be work, but after that I get to be a grownup kid hanging with her adult friends. While on this flight, I have already written three devotions, and this is the shorter leg of the trip. This flight is only one hour and forty-five minutes long. Half an hour into the flight, the pilot announces that there is quite a bit of turbulence ahead. Control towers are currently rerouting our flight. He says this all while putting great emphasis on the importance of staying seated with our seatbelts fastened. If it should clear, we would have the opportunity to get up and move about in the cabin. This is the first time in my travel history we have been confined to our designated seats. Dare at your own risk if you must waddle to the lavatory. The pilot resends his first announcement with newfound information: he's just been informed by the air traffic control tower that there is a storm in Mississippi and another in New Orleans. My destination is Atlanta, Georgia. Then he said, "We are between two complexes. While it is going to be a rough ride, these storms provide us with tailwinds that aid in getting us to our gates with an early arrival time."

Some storms, as I'm learning, are necessary. There are lessons to be learned all around us, we just need to keep our eyes, ears, hearts, and minds open to receive them. The interesting thing about this revelation for me is that oftentimes, if I have my earphones on, I rarely take them off for anything, let alone another turbulent announcement, but today was different. Because I was in expectation, I needed to do something different. My willingness to change taught me this great truth: For you to get to your appointed destination, you may experience a few complexities. God is the author and the finisher. He knows just how much turbulence is needed to get our attention. I heard this quote this week, "A diamond is a piece of coal that endured pressures differently." Carry on, it's only a process.

"This turbulence worked in our favor."

ALL ELSE IS A LIE

1 THESSALONIANS 5:24 (NLT)

God will make this happen,
for he who calls you is faithful.

SOME *Things Made Plain* was a God idea. He downloaded into my spirit to write pen to paper His ideas about His Word. The beginning of this project would have me fluttering all over the place, writing in my sleep on sheets. Sticky notes were posted all over the place. Someone on television would say something and, suddenly, I had something to write about.

I should have told myself from the start, "Theresa do not listen to the haters." Someone said to me, "Why are you still writing?" I was on my third book by this time. "Why don't you wait 'til your name is noticeable?" At first, I ignored the comments, but then the book sales slowed down, and I had fewer speaking engagements to promote the project. Boom! Just like that, I fell into a writer's slump. Then the day happened when I heard the Holy Spirit remind me this was not a Theresa idea, this was a God idea, *"ALL ELSE IS A LIE."* He was clearly telling me He does not quit anything He starts, so I don't have that option either. I am created in His image, so I've got His DNA. The revelation was twofold when I thought I was in a writer's slump. He was still talking, I had just stopped listening. When God speaks, it is always for a purpose. If I had shut out the chatter of the haters, this project would have been finished earlier.

Willa, my publisher, would encourage me by saying, "When it is supposed to be complete, it will be." Well, here it is. The journey has been great. I am not the same person I was when I started *Some Things Made Plain.* I have gained many great nuggets, but the greatest of them all is there is never any good reason to stop doing what God said. The revelation of this scripture is this one truth: If He called you to do it, He will not forfeit His character by not allowing it to be completed, because it is Him completing this work through us. When the Father chooses you to be the vessel on the earth to complete an assignment that could potentially change lives, He's with you all the way to the finish line. He faithfully completes all that He started, even the work in us, through us, for us.

"The covenant keeper obligates Himself to complete all He has begun."

MAKE IT COUNT

Psalms 116:1-2 (NASB)

I love the LORD, because He hears My voice and my supplications. Because He has inclined His ear to me, Therefore I shall call upon Him as long as I live.

Volume 4 is complete—this is the last book of the series. Tomorrow just happens to be my 50th birthday. I never get emotional regarding birthdays. I always say the old cliché, "Age is just a number," but this one hit me a little differently. Yesterday, in a group text with some of my very good friends, I let them in on where I was mentally. They all quickly responded with words of encouragement, saying things like "Fifty is the new fabulous," "This is when you really start living," or "Your boldness gets wiser." I told them that I was working on getting this manuscript to my publisher by the end of the day.

My phone quickly rang; it was my friend Donna. I burst into tears. I began to express this is not how I saw my life at 50—divorced after 31 years. I should be traveling, seeing the world. Our children aren't children, after all. However, I then reminded myself why I had made the decision. It had been one heartbreak too many. Donna listened to my heart that day. A few beautiful words of encouragement later, she said, "Make this monumental birthday count. Turn your manuscript in tomorrow. On your birthday, give a birthday gift to yourself."

Life changes are inevitable. Be that as it may, our peace of mind is solely up to us, based on the choices we make. In my case, not being secure in my relationship was affecting many areas in my life. I stopped writing. I wasn't taking care of my temple. I had become a recluse. I was merely going through the motions but not fully living. I decided to seek peace and pursue it to start living again, to make every day count. I reminded myself, I am here on purpose. With this change in my heart and mind my gloomy days were fewer. I became the center of my attention, my focus was back on my destiny, and Jesus was now healing the areas I was pretending did not hurt. Oh, how I love Him! All I needed to do was allow Him to do what He does best—mend the brokenhearted. If you find yourself disagreeing with the inevitable, tell yourself this: "I am here on purpose for a purpose." Then, make all your days count, just be mindful to take the One who cares the most for you along. He made your days and wants them all to count, so do not be discouraged. God is near listening to every prayer with excitement to answer and give you His very best.

"He made the day with you in mind. Make it count."

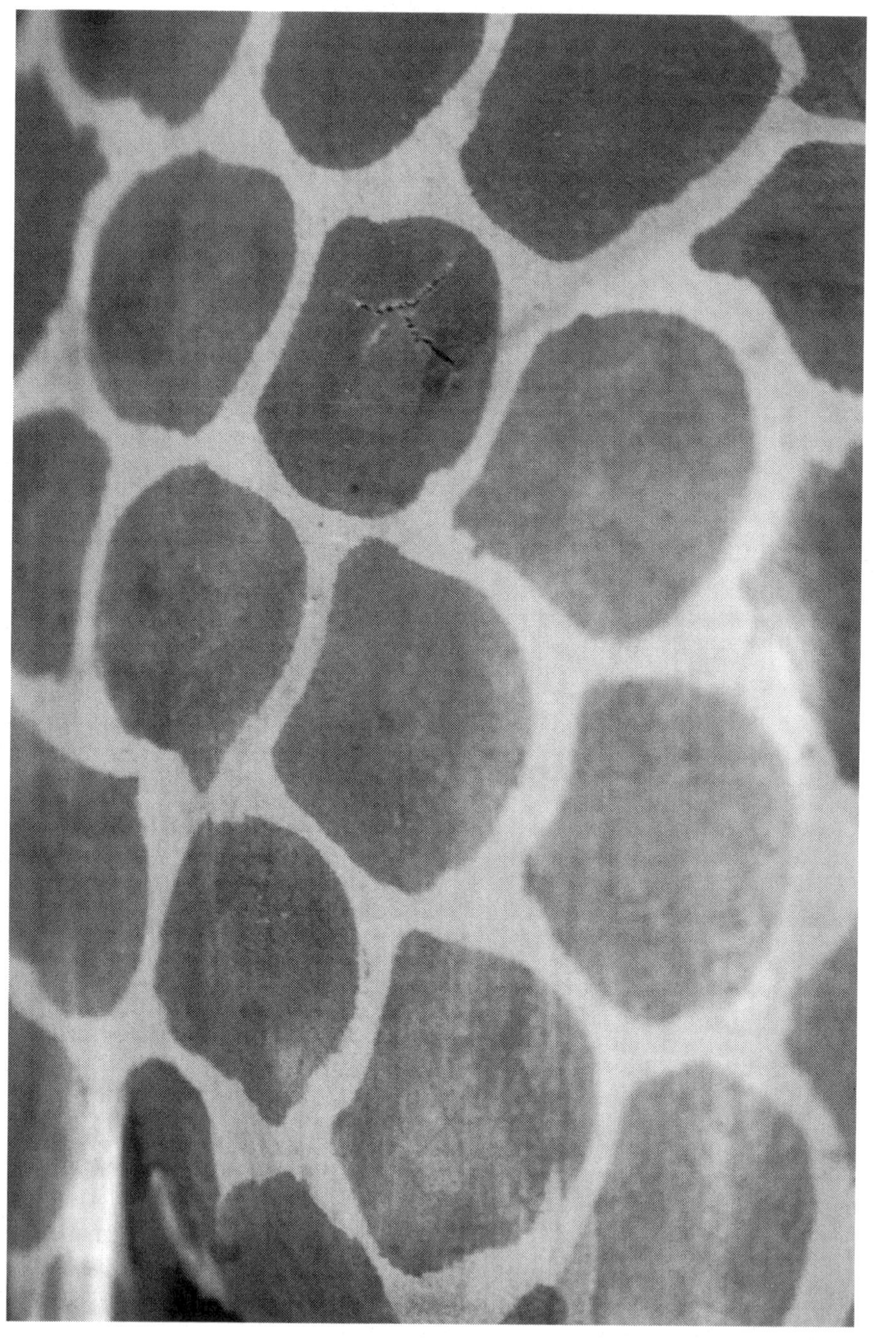

EARNEST SALVATION

JOHN 3:16 (KJV)

For God so loved the world, that he gave his only begotten Son, that whosoever believeth in him should not perish, but have everlasting life.

Earnest: seriously important; demanding or receiving serious attention

Salvation: the act of saving or protecting from harm, risk, loss, destruction

WHEN purchasing a home, you must have what is called "earnest money." This is money set aside to prove you can be trusted, you are serious, and you have thought about this purchase. You are about to make a lifetime commitment. Even when the home is totally paid for, you still have the maintenance of it. Where there is a commitment, there must be action. The action you put forth is the commitment to care for and provide the things needed for the home. Jesus on the Cross is God's earnest money for our souls. He was set aside to show us that God can be trusted, and His action of obedience is only a test—a pledge of His love and commitment to us. We can trust Him for eternal life. Jesus on the Cross is God's promise that there is more to come, and it is heaven. Heaven is where He has provided an atmosphere of angels who praise and worship Him only because of who He is. Heaven is a place of perfect health, no stress, no fear, no lacks... all peace, praise, protection, and provision. For all have sinned and fallen short of the glory of God. However, we are justified by His grace as a gift, through the redemption that is in Christ Jesus. Man is sinful. The result of sin is death. It is spiritual separation from God. Jesus died in our place, so we can live with Him forever. We can't earn Salvation through our works; we are saved by God's grace when we have faith in His son Jesus Christ.

"This earnest money is Redemption at its greatest work."

PRAYER OF SALVATION

ROMANS 10:9 (KJV)

*That if thou shalt confess with thy mouth the Lord Jesus,
and shalt believe in thine heart that God hath raised him from the dead,
thou shalt be saved.*

FATHER, I confess that I am a sinner. I ask that you come into my heart and save me, that you give me the opportunity to live eternally with you. I recognize that Jesus Christ is your only begotten son, that He willfully died for my sins that I may be cleansed from all unrighteousness. Lord, I thank you for my salvation and for your grace and daily mercies. You are awesome to love me as you do, and for this I will bless your name forever. Create in me a new heart, and renew a steadfast spirit within me that I may live an acceptable life that will be pleasing to you until you return. As I rejoice for my new life, I understand that all the angels in heaven rejoice along with me. Jesus, thank you for the Blood that from this moment will cover my life and keep me safe from the snares of the wicked one. *Amen.*

CORINTHIANS 6:2 (KJV)

*For he saith, I have heard thee in a time accepted,
and in the day of salvation have I succoured thee:
behold, now is the accepted time;
behold, now is the day of salvation.*

AMEN

Revelation 3:14 (AMP)

And to the angel (messenger) of the assembly (church) in Laodicea write: These are the words of the Amen, the trusty and faithful and true Witness, the Origin and beginning and Author of God's creation

Avenger ~ 1 Thessalonians 4:6 (AMP)

That no man transgress and overreach his brother and defraud him in this matter or defraud his brother in business. For the Lord is an avenger in all these things, as we have already warned you solemnly and told you plainly.

Abba ~ Romans 9:15 (NKJV)

For you did not receive the spirit of bondage again to fear, but you received the Spirit of adoption by whom we cry out, "Abba, Father."

Advocate ~ 1 John 2:1 (NKJV)

My little children, these things I write to you, so that you may not sin. And if anyone sins, we have an Advocate with the Father, Jesus Christ the righteous.

Almighty ~ Genesis 17:1 (NKJV)

When Abram was ninety-nine years old, the Lord appeared to Abram and said to him, "I am Almighty God; walk before Me and be blameless."

All in All ~ Colossians 3:11 (NKJV)

where there is neither Greek nor Jew, circumcised nor uncircumcised, barbarian, Scythian, slave nor free, but Christ is all and in all.

Ancient of Days ~ Daniel 7:9 (NIV)

As I looked, "thrones were set in place, and the Ancient of Days took his seat. His clothing was as white as snow; the hair of his head was white like wool. His throne was flaming with fire, and its wheels were all ablaze.

Author of Eternal Salvation ~ Hebrews 5:9 (NIV)

...and, once made perfect, he became the source of eternal salvation for all who obey him

Author of Our Faith ~ Hebrews 12:2 (NIV)

...fixing our eyes on Jesus, the pioneer and perfection of faith. For the joy set before him he endured the cross, scorning its shame, and sat down at the right hand of the throne of God.

Amen

ABOUT THE AUTHOR

Theresa Kirk is an ordained minister, teacher of the gospel of Jesus Christ, published author of four books, motivational speaker, mentor, and coach. While writing this volume, Minister Theresa, as she is affectionately known, made a lifestyle change to live a healthier life, experiencing great success, and confirming the revelation that our bodies are the temple of the Holy Ghost. She has inspired and assisted many who have changed their life with what she coins as "Healthy Habits." Minister Theresa believes that God has given her the gift of revelation and knowledge to complete the last volume, *It's That Simple.* The four-book series, *Some Things Made Plain,* inspires readers to take the time to read the Word of God. Her mission is for readers to understand that the Word is *SIMPLE,* full of compassion and yet it is loaded with power that God himself has endorsed for us to use while we are still here on earth. She is a gifted speaker utilizing wisdom, knowledge, coupled with humor to captivate her listeners and always welcomes the Holy Spirit to every teaching.

Minister Theresa speaks at Christian conferences and retreats throughout the United States. She is a cabinet leader for the women's ministry at her church, Living Praise Christian Center, at the Chatsworth, California campus, under the leadership of Pastors, Dr. Fred L. and Linda G. Hodge. Minister Theresa is a teacher at Living Praise Christian Institute, a comprehensive school of ministry. She is the mother of two beautiful adult children, Chelsea and Jaylon, and resides in Valencia, California.

REFERENCES

King James Version (KJV)
New King James Version (NKJV)
English Standard Version (ESV)
New International Version (NIV)
Message (MSG)
Amplified Version (AMP)
Contemporary English Version (CEV)
Gods Word Translation (GWT)
Holman Christian Standard Bible (HCSB)
New Living Translation (NLT)
New Century Version (NCV)
Today's New International Version (TNIV)
International Standard Version (ISV)
Dictionary.com, LLC. Copyright @ 2016 Roget's College Thesaurus

Made in the USA
San Bernardino, CA
13 October 2017